Nine Months to a Miracle

MARI HANES

HARVEST HOUSE PUBLISHERS

EUGENE, OREGON

Cover by Koechel Peterson & Associates, Inc., Minneapolis, Minnesota

Cover photo © Kaycee Craig/iStockphoto

NINE MONTHS TO A MIRACLE
Copyright © 1979 by Mari Hanes
Published by Harvest House Publishers
Eugene, Oregon 97402
www.harvesthousepublishers.com

Library of Congress Cataloging-in-Publication Data
Hanes, Mari.
 Nine months to a miracle / Mari Hanes.—[Rev. and updated ed.].
  p. cm.
 Rev. ed. of: The child within. c1979.
 Includes bibliographical references.
  ISBN-13: 978-0-7369-1808-4 (pbk.)
  ISBN-10: 0-7369-1808-6
 1. Pregnant women—Prayer-books and devotions—English. I. Hanes, Mari. Child within. II. Title.
 BV4847.H36 2006
 242.'6431—dc22   2006004897

Printed in the United States of America

   06 07 08 09 10 11 12 13 14 / VP-CF / 10 9 8 7 6 5 4 3 2 1

As the child developing within you and your spirit are both nourished during pregnancy, God sets certain laws in motion. Growth is natural and inevitable.

These months before delivery can add a quality to your life that will always remain with you.

For Sara Lace, Ben, Sam, Nora,
and all the grandbabies to come…

Contents

Foreword
7

Conception
11

The First Month
Conceiving and Receiving
13

The Second Month
A Spiritual Embryo
31

The Third Month
Free from Fear
49

The Fourth Month
A Study in Stability
63

The Fifth Month
In Control
77

The Sixth Month

The Gift of Sight

93

The Seventh Month

Preparing a Home

111

The Eighth Month

Refining and Reflection

127

Delivery

My Great Physician

141

The Newborn

The Feminine Side of God

159

Bibliography

173

FOREWORD

I have had six pregnancies. Each one was different, and during each one I discovered new treasures and new wisdom from Scripture.

More than 25 years ago, I gathered my thoughts into a Bible study for expectant mothers (*The Child Within*, published by Tyndale House Publishers). As that book continued to be reprinted and translated into other languages, I was overwhelmed by the commonality of the responses from women of many cultures and many nations. I have wonderful letters translated from Mandarin Chinese and Swahili and even Afrikaans.

In an article in *Good Housekeeping* magazine, singer Debbie Boone Ferrar wrote, "Besides dealing with the physical fears for my unborn babies that women have faced from the beginning of time, I am dealing with a world more troubled and unsure than ever. Before giving birth to my twins, I found the greatest comfort in reading Mari Hanes' book and learning I am not alone in my emotions and the fears I am fighting."

She was echoing the truth from 2 Peter 5:9 that is almost humorous if we paraphrase it in reference to pregnancy: "There has come upon you *no strange affliction* that is different than that experienced by others in this season."

God is with us in every season. How grateful I am for the editors at Harvest House Publishers and their desire to publish this new, totally updated study, *Nine Months to a Miracle*. We hurried to complete the book so that my daughter and daughters-in-law could use it during their precious seasons of days-in-waiting.

More important than the words of this simple book are the things God will speak to your heart about the unique and special child within you. May you be like Mary, the mother of Jesus, who "pondered all these things in her heart."

And may you be surprised with a pregnancy that is one of the happiest and most fulfilling seasons of your life.

There are days in your pregnancy
   when your heart fills with the warmth of joy
      and, like the flight of a pastel balloon,
         seems to float into heaven.

Your thrill at the thought of life within
   is swallowed by the even greater anticipation
      of who that little life will be.
         But there are other days—
            thankfully fewer—
         when physical and emotional pressures
            combine to rob you
         of your happiness and peace.
      It is for those days that this study guide
         is written.

Find comfort in knowing that your fears and
  worries are neither strange,
    nor unusual...
Just as every healthy fetus develops
    according to a certain physical pattern,
every expectant mother
    has in common with her sisters
      the need for many steps of inner growth
As your baby develops physically within you,
  may you develop emotional and spiritual stability.
    Most of all,
      may you learn to draw on the enduring
      strength of a heavenly Father
      who promises to...

Gently lead those who are with young.

ISAIAH 40:11

Conception

Great is our Lord, and mighty in power:

His understanding is infinite.

The Lord is good to all,

and His tender mercies are over all His works.

Let them praise the name of the Lord:

for He commanded and they were created.

PSALM 147:5; 145:9; 148:5

The First Month

The most important and amazing development of the embryo takes place before a woman even confirms with her physician that she is pregnant: A story has begun that is so remarkable that no novelist or scientist could have imagined it. A sperm, one of some 500 million released during intercourse, has united with an egg snuggled deep within your body. At that instant, your baby's sex, hair color, and eye color are determined. Within the first few days, the embryo has more than 200 cells, which from the beginning are uniquely human. Just as you will prepare a home for your family, your body makes a home for your child before birth. Blood levels of progesterone and other hormones in your body rise quickly, and you notice the changes. By the end of the first month, the embryo's spinal cord and heart are forming. The digestive system and sensory systems are being created. Small buds appear that will soon become arms and legs. A new human being is on the way, and your own life will never be the same.

You covered me in my mother's womb.

I will praise You, for I am

fearfully and wonderfully made...

My frame was not hidden from You,

When I was made in secret...

And in Your book they

all were written,

The days fashioned for me.

PSALM 139:13-16

CONCEIVING AND RECEIVING

In everything give thanks; for this is the
will of God in Christ Jesus for you.
1 THESSALONIANS 5:18

Babies are conceived under many different circumstances.

Some pregnancies are the result of months of planning and prayer that culminate in conception, bringing tremendous joy to both parents. Some pregnancies bring unexpected delight and are as wonderfully surprising as an early Christmas would be to a four-year-old. Other pregnancies are not only unplanned but also unwanted, and for many valid reasons they may fill the expectant mother's heart with dread and fear.

Whether you conceived purposefully or not, you must settle one question in these first weeks: *Is this child a part of God's will for my life?*

The Bible's answer to your question will flood your heart with peace: Your child was not conceived outside of the foreknowledge of your heavenly Father. God's words to your unborn infant are the same as His words to the prophet Jeremiah: "I knew you before you were formed within your mother's womb" (Jeremiah 1:5 TLB).

From the moment you know a child is forming within you, you can receive that tiny being as part of God's will for your life. And His will, contrary to what many have thought, is a plan designed to bring about your *greatest happiness.* Have you had misgivings about God's blueprint for your life, secretly dreading what He may bring your way? If so, 1 John 4:18 may illuminate the reason:

> We need have no fear of someone who loves us perfectly; his perfect love for us eliminates all dread of what he might do to us. If we are afraid, it is for fear of what he might do to us and shows that we are not fully convinced that he really loves us (TLB).

Even if you have heard about a loving heavenly Father since you were a child, you may not be fully convinced that He really loves you *individually* and *unconditionally.* During pregnancy, perhaps more than at any other time of your life, you need to be *fully convinced* of His love. You need to rest in that love, allowing it to be the stabilizing factor for your life and for the life of your family.

The message of God's love for each of us flashes like a neon light throughout the Bible, and we must "believe him when he tells us that he loves us dearly" (1 John 4:16 TLB). Understanding that God wants the best for you will enable you to believe the promise of His Word that "all that happens to us is working for our good if we love God and are fitting into his plans" (Romans 8:28 TLB).

During pregnancy, changing hormones may place you on an emotional trampoline; at times you may not feel that God (or anyone else) really loves you. (The amount of some hormones in your system may triple!) But remember, we don't base our faith on our feelings but on the Bible's assurance of His love for us. In 2 Corinthians 5:7 Paul tells us, "We walk by faith, not by sight." That means our spiritual life is not based on our senses and feelings, which are inconsistent, but on God's Word, which is eternal and unchanging. You can be certain that this pregnancy flowed from the hand of the One who loves you and who also loves the child forming within you.

Concerns About Our World

You may have been hesitant to bring a baby into such a troubled world. Television, news reports, magazines, and books broadcast a fearful message of impending doom. Many women today are afraid to have children because they are concerned about what the future holds for them.

Christians are not immune to this fear. As believers, we understand that Christ has promised to return to earth, but He also warns us of "wars and rumors of wars." Environmentalists point out the effect the world's population has on nature. Media showcase the breakdown of family values and the dangers of drugs and alcohol and communicable disease. A young woman can easily begin to carry silent but very real worries about the future.

Dread of the future should never be a reason for Christians to remain childless! Scriptural principles are timeless, and Jeremiah 29:5-6 highlights God's enduring attitude about having children. Even as His own children faced foreign exile in Babylon, the Holy Spirit spoke through the prophet and gave these instructions:

> Build homes and plan to stay; plant vineyards...Marry and have children, and then find mates for them and have many grandchildren. Multiply! Don't dwindle away! (TLB).

Then, in verse 11, God explained why we can look to the future with confidence:

> "For I know the plans I have for you," says the Lord. "They are plans for good and not for evil, to give you a future and a hope" (TLB).

This Scripture assures God's children of two things:

1. He wants us to experience the joy of having families, and
2. He will bless and keep our families in any world situation we may face.

Christian couples may have valid reasons for not having children, but fear is not one of them. We should not make decisions based on fear.

The Wonder of "God's Book"

DNA. Deoxyribonucleic acid. In 1953 in Cambridge, England, scientists isolated the fundamental molecule of life. Every normal human cell (including each cell of your embryo from the moment of conception), contains 46 chromosomes of genetic material. Half of this material is provided by the father and half by the mother. The DNA in each cell looks like a microscopic spiral staircase.

DNA is like a tiny computer, miniaturized beyond Intel's wildest dreams. Programmed into its data bank is an almost inconceivable amount of information that spells out the biological and chemical functions of life. A single thread of DNA located in just one human cell may house enough information to fill *1000 volumes, each 600 pages thick!*

God's book! (See Psalm 139:16.)

Concerns About Past Pregnancies

The Word of God has comfort and wisdom for every situation a woman can face.

Have You Known the Heartbreak of Miscarriage?

> We do not have a High Priest who cannot sympathize with our weaknesses (Hebrews 4:15).

Following a very painful miscarriage, I looked for the word *miscarriage* in the Bible but couldn't find it. I discovered Scripture uses other terms.

In the book of Job, one of the most ancient of biblical texts, we read that "a stillborn child…who never saw light" will be with the "kings and counselors of the earth…the small and great" (see Job 3:9-19).

The Old Testament shows that a miscarried child is not eternally lost to us. Remember Psalm 139:16? "In Your book they were all written, the days fashioned for me." When scientists looked into a microscope in 1953 and first identified spiraling strands of DNA like those in each human embryo from conception, they were seeing God's book. I believe that in miscarriage, that book of blueprints can be developed in the heavenly kingdom. (In my case, the blueprint of the tiny boy [and later twins] that I miscarried will probably give them the marble blue eyes and almost-bald heads of the three healthy babies I carried full term.)

Some 400,000 women experience the pain of miscarriage each year in the United States alone. Physicians tell us that by far most spontaneous miscarriages occur because the blueprint was not developing properly.

More infrequently, however, obstetricians may discover treat-able conditions: anatomical abnormalities such as adhesions in the uterus (myomas), infections such as T-strain mycoplasmas, or even hormonal needs.

Many promises in Scripture directly apply to miscarriage. In Psalm 113:9 (TLB), we read, "He gives children to the childless wife, so that she becomes a happy mother." In Genesis 49:25, we read that women can ask for "blessings of the breasts and of the womb." In fact, if you take time to count the people who experienced physical healings in both the Old and New Testaments, the largest group were women who were longing to have a baby!

Some fear about pregnancy is normal after miscarriage. But this fear should not paralyze us or hold us back from the joy of having children. If a previous pregnancy brought miscarriage, take a moment to write the following verses in your own words:

Genesis 49:25

_____

_____

_____

_____

Psalm 128:3

_____

_____

_____

_____

*Sing, O barren, you who have not
borne! Break forth into singing.*

ISAIAH 54:1

*He gives children to the childless wife,
so that she becomes
a happy mother! Hallelujah!*

PSALM 113:9 (TLB)

God Knows

Your heavenly Father knows the baby inside you, and He is intimately involved in knitting that child together. Your heavenly Father knows *you,* and His Spirit can be with you in every season of life. And in addition to knowing your child and knowing you, He clearly knows your situation. He knows if you have health concerns. He knows if you are worried about insurance and medical bills. He knows if you are insecure about your ability to be a good parent.

This month is a wonderful time to discover one of the Old Testament's names for the Creator. In Genesis 16 we read the touching story of a pregnant woman who was lost in the wilderness. Her name was Hagar, and her little child would be named Ishmael. Hagar was in complete despair about her pregnancy and about her future. But then she was surprised by the presence of God, who comforted her and gave her hope for her future. And Hagar called her Creator by a name that has endured for centuries and is loved by both Jews and Christians. That name is *El Roi*—"the God Who Sees Me."

Have You Known the Regret of Abortion?

Women with unwanted pregnancies have often been guided toward abortion. Many young women receive pressure from the biological father of the embryo, from parents, or from medical professionals. Other women make the choice purely out of fear or because they don't believe the pregnancy really produced a tiny life. Thousands of women later experience regret and guilt, and those are some of the most tortuous and draining of all human feelings. Regret and guilt cause us to suffer emotionally as well as spiritually. The only answer, and the reason that Jesus "became flesh and dwelt among us" (John l:14), is that "He was wounded and bruised for our sins" (Isaiah 53:5 TLB).

In Lamentations 1:16 (TLB), Jeremiah calls God a Comforter. And God instructs the prophet Isaiah to "Speak comfort to Jerusalem…that her warfare [her struggle] is ended, that her iniquity is pardoned" (Isaiah 40:2).

Please don't carry regret or guilt into this new pregnancy. Take time now not only to copy the powerful and freeing promise from Isaiah, but to memorize it as well.

_____

_____

At this crucial time in your life, will you allow the Holy Spirit to *fully convince* you of His love for you and for your child? Will you understand that He is *El Roi,* the God Who Sees Me? Will you embrace His love with your heart and not just with your mind?

Before you begin the following study, go to your Father in honest prayer. Hebrews 4:15-16 urges you to approach Him without fear. Your relationship with Him is dearly intimate; you may call Him "Abba, Father" (Romans 8:15), and the best interpretation of the Greek word *abba* would be "daddy" or "papa"!

Ask the Lord to give you the confidence that the embryo snuggled deep inside of you is a part of His wonderful plan for your life. Next, ask Him to assure you that He also has a wonderful plan for the child He is knitting together. Then you will experience a surge of thankfulness for the priceless gift of the child inside you.

Behold, children are a heritage of the LORD,
The fruit of the womb is a reward.

PSALM 127:3

$\mathscr{F}$AITH $\mathscr{B}$UILDERS

I Can Trust in God's Love
Study 1 John 4:9-10. What is the greatest way in which God has shown His love for you?

_____

Have you received the gift of God's love by receiving His Son, Jesus Christ, as your personal Savior?_____ "If you confess with your mouth the Lord Jesus and believe in your heart that God has raised Him from the dead, you will be saved" (Romans 10:9).

The Lord Jesus not only loves you, He understands you perfectly! How is He able to do this? (Read Hebrews 4:15.)

_____

_____

Sometimes, even after we become part of God's family, we feel like hiding from Him because of sin. Your intimate relationship with your heavenly Father can be immediately restored. How? (Read 1 John 1:9.)

_____

You never need to feel far from God's love!

I Can Trust in God's Will

As a child of God, you are eager to discover His plan for your life, for you know that God's love flows out of His wisdom. What does Isaiah 55:8-9 teach us about the wisdom of God and our own plans and decisions?

_____

_____

How does James 1:17 describe the things God wants to bring your way?

_____

Isaiah 55 teaches the joy of living in the will of the Lord. Read verses 12 and 13 and list some of the benefits and blessings you find.

_____

_____

If you are a mother-to-be who is single or separated from your husband, your pregnancy may have caused deep anxiety. Discover the Lord's special promise to become your Comforter, Counselor, and Protector. Read Isaiah 54:4-8 and note God's promises to you.

_____

I Can Trust in God's Ways

Think about the privilege of pregnancy. Read Genesis 4:1 and name the source of your ability to conceive.

_____

God's plan for man's earthly happiness centers around what unit? (See Psalm 128:3-4).

_____

Your ability to help fashion a new being is an awesome gift from God. It may be the way in which you are most like Him. Write a few sentences, thanking God for the gift of this child and affirming your trust that His will for you is good.

_____

_____

_____

A Thought to Ponder

The New Testament uses the Greek word *brephos* for both an unborn baby and a newborn infant. When pregnant Elizabeth, the mother of John the Baptist, met Mary, the *brephos* within her leapt for joy (Luke 1:41). Later, Mary wrapped her *brephos* (Jesus) in swaddling clothes and laid Him in a manger (Luke 2:7).

The tiny embryo within you is already a baby in God's eyes!

𝒻urther 𝒟evotional ℛeading

God Loves Me

> I have loved you with an everlasting love;
> Therefore with lovingkindness I have drawn you
> (Jeremiah 31:3).

Also see Deuteronomy 7:8; John 3:16; 13:1; 15:13; 16:27; Romans 5:8; 8:35; Ephesians 2:4-5; 1 John 3:1

My Child Is a Blessing from God...a Reward!

> Children are a heritage from the LORD,
> The fruit of the womb is a reward (Psalm 127:3).

Also see Genesis 33:5; 48:9; Joshua 24:3; Psalm 113:9; 127:5; 128:3; Proverbs 17:6; Isaiah 8:18

God Is Forming My Child

> You formed my inward parts;
> You covered me in my mother's womb (Psalm 139:13).

Also see Job 10:8-12; 31:15; Psalm 119:73; 139:14-16; Ecclesiastes 11:5; Isaiah 42:5; 43:7; 44:2,21,24; 49:5; Zechariah 12:1; Malachi 2:10; Acts 17:24-28; Colossians 1:16-17; Revelation 4:11

SUMMARY

As you trust that God will use your pregnancy in His wonderful and eternal plan for your life, you can *thankfully accept* the gift of the child forming within you. As you commit your life and your baby's life to the Lord, He can let "all things work together for good"! You will develop emotionally as the baby in your uterus develops physically.

Welcome to what can be the greatest experience of your life!

Things
My Doctor
Told Me This Month...

_____

_____

_____

_____

_____

_____

My Physical Changes...

_____

_____

_____

Things
I've Thought
About This Month...

_____

_____

_____

_____

_____

_____

My Special Verse...

_____

_____

_____

The Second Month

The embryo is now one and an eighth inches long but weighs only a tenth of an ounce. Limbs begin to show clear divisions into legs, feet, arms, and hands as soft bones are forming. The umbilical cord is distinctly visible. Internal organs are developing, especially the digestive system. Face and features begin to form, but the eyelids are fused shut. Blood vessels and the heart are developing, and the heart is faintly beating.

As you do not know what

is the way of the wind,

Or how the bones grow in the

womb of her who is with child,

So you do not know the works of

God who makes everything.

ECCLESIASTES 11:5

A SPIRITUAL EMBRYO

Being confident of this very thing, that He
who has begun a good work in you will
complete it until the day of Jesus Christ.

PHILIPPIANS 1:6

By six weeks your pregnancy has been easily confirmed by a visit to your doctor. You now have medical confirmation that, in your excitement, you have not just imagined the baby growing inside you.

However you made your earthshaking announcement, the word is out. Snuggled deep within the safety of your uterus, a tiny person is now forming! Close friends hug you in congratulations, neighbors ask if you want a boy or a girl, and perhaps your mother-in-law breathes a contented, "Well, finally!"

Perhaps you feel like pinning a note to your still flat and inconspicuous tummy that says, "An Announcement: A Baby Is in Here!" You have officially joined the ranks of the women in waiting. Your heart sings as you go through your days, "In seven and a half months I will be a mother! In seven and a half months we will be three instead of two. In seven and a half months..." Suddenly you pause mid sentence as concern cascades over your excitement. The nine-month gestation period, which once sounded so long, is now clearly a very short time in which to prepare yourself for parenthood. Your body must be ready for labor and delivery, and your heart must be ready as well.

Preparing to bring an infant into your home includes myriad details. As a Christian believer, you recognize that life is not only physical, it is spiritual. Your heart cries out, *O God, when I see my spiritual and emotional development as a parent, I am as incomplete as the embryo within me!*

This recognition of spiritual need is your only prerequisite for spiritual growth. Jesus promised in Matthew 7:7 that if we seek, we will find, and if we knock at His door, He will open it for us. As you accept that you need God to develop your own character and maturity while His laws of nature are developing your baby, He will be free to do just that! The Word promises that He always hears the cry of a sincere heart (Psalm 34:17; 55:17; 145:19; Isaiah 30:19).

Philippians 1:6 is a wonderful verse for every expectant mother. The Living Bible says it in this way: "God who began the good work within you will keep right on helping you grow in his grace until his task within you is finally finished."

As soon as we commit our lives to God, He *does* begin a good work in us! Don't be impatient with yourself just because you fail to reach spiritual maturity overnight. That would be as unnatural as having a baby that learned to walk and run in a few days! James 1:4 urges you to "let patience have its perfect work, that you may be perfect and complete, lacking nothing." You must be patient with yourself, for your loving heavenly Father is patient with you. He is full of gracious compassion, slow to anger, and great in mercy (Psalm 145:8).

The crucial question is whether or not you are spiritually hungry. (By the way, aren't you surprised to feel the physical hunger brought on by the embryo you cannot yet see?) You shouldn't ask yourself, *Am I full-grown spiritually?* but rather, *Am I spiritually hungry so that I will keep on growing?* The Amplified Bible's rendering of 1 Peter 3:11 urges us to pursue peaceful relations with God.

To ensure that growth, you will need a great deal of spiritual nourishment. During your pregnancy, your medical professional will give you advice about the food, liquid, and vitamins and minerals you will need. A well-balanced diet will meet all the nutritional needs of your developing baby. The wise woman will decide to follow this advice carefully. Your diet affects not only your baby's health but may also affect his or her intelligence in some ways. The wise woman will also realize that her spirit, like the vulnerable embryo, is nourished continually. God has provided three nutrients for spiritual growth, and these nutrients work together to weave a strong strand of spiritual DNA.

Building Blocks of Spiritual DNA
The Milk of the Word

A newborn baby draws all of its needs from one substance: milk. Physicians have verified that milk, especially a mother's milk, provides a perfectly balanced diet for the tiny infant. Scripture draws a parallel to this perfect diet:

> As newborn babes, desire the pure milk of the word,
> that you may grow thereby (1 Peter 2:2).

The Word of God provides a perfectly balanced diet for your spirit. "The whole Bible was given to us by inspiration from God and is useful to teach us what is true and to make us realize what is wrong in our lives...It is God's way of making us well prepared at every point" (2 Timothy 3:16-17 TLB). Prepared even for motherhood.

One of the most common traits in pregnant women is hunger—even a *craving* for certain things to eat or drink. The medical term for this is *pica*. This, in fact, is one of the first ways some women know they are expecting: They have unusual cravings! Before the uterus even begins to grow, the pregnant body is desperate for nourishment. Every family jokes about how an expectant mother just *had* to have pizza with sausage and olives or a strawberry-banana milkshake in the middle of the night! And, as every wise married man has learned, these cravings are not to be ignored!

In John 4:10,14, Jesus compares His words to living water. He tells the woman at the well that He can give her living water that will quench her spiritual thirst. In John 6:35,48, He calls Himself the Bread of Life and tells us that if we take in His words, our spiritual cravings and hunger will be satisfied.

One of the saddest sights in the world is that of a grown woman who, because of accident or illness, has lost the use of her muscles and cannot even feed herself. Equally sad is seeing a woman starving with anorexia, who doesn't eat even when good food is in front of her. And God is just as sad when He sees one of His daughters who does not know how to feed her spirit. We cannot receive enough spiritual nourishment from the few verses our pastor may read on Sunday morning, just as we cannot maintain a healthy pregnancy by eating once a week! And the Bible's verses that deal with pregnancy and motherhood and feminine strength could never all be covered in public services.

God has put a special blessing on His Word; children can understand it, and yet the world's wisest teachers continue to find treasure in its wisdom. And in this generation, we are privileged to have the Bible in so many remarkable translations. Some prefer the New King James, others the New International Version. The Living Bible uses words that often speak right to a pregnant woman's heart. Another paraphrase that brings new insight into many verses is The Message.

Only you can watch over your diet to see that your baby gets all the physical nourishment it needs in these nine months of growth, and only you can make sure you receive all the spiritual nourishment you need.

The Strength of Prayer

You may be kneeling or washing dishes, you may whisper or speak loudly, or you may close your eyes and pray mentally as you lay your head on your pillow each night. The question is, are you talking to your Father each day? Throughout Scripture we are taught to "call upon Him while He is near" (Isaiah 55:6).

No one needs to face any of the concerns of pregnancy or the responsibilities of parenting alone. "Don't worry about anything; instead, pray about everything; tell God your needs, and don't forget to thank him for his answers" (Philippians 4:6 TLB). In prayer you have the privilege of talking to the all-powerful God, who had the authority to speak the universe into existence. But you also have the privilege of talking to the understanding Savior. Remember the verses in Hebrews we saw in chapter 1?

> This High Priest of ours understands our weaknesses since he had the same temptations we do, though he never once gave way to them and sinned. So let us come boldly to the very throne of God and stay there to receive his

mercy and to find grace to help us in our times of need (Hebrews 4:15-16 TLB).

In Philippians 4:6, Paul encourages us, "With thanksgiving, let your requests be made known to God." Take a moment to put into writing your thankfulness for the gift of the new baby you have been given:

_____

_____

_____

_____

Each day, for the rest of this pregnancy, you can begin your prayer with those words of sincere thanksgiving.

Friendship with Other Believers

> But if we are living in the light of God's presence, just as Christ does, then we have wonderful fellowship and joy with each other (1 John 1:7 TLB).

God's will is for you to be part of a local church family. When the Word speaks of fellowship, it means much more than sitting in a church service or knowing other believers only on a "hello...goodbye" basis. Especially during this season in your life, you need to have a vital, living relationship with the body of Christ. This isn't always easy, especially in our highly mobile culture, but it is an important goal. "All of you together are the one body of Christ, and each one of you is a separate and necessary part of it" (1 Corinthians 12:27 TLB).

If you lack true and deep Christian fellowship, tell your Father your need. Ask Him to add to your life dear friends who will give you the godly encouragement and support you need as a young wife and mother.

Some surveys have shown that as many as two out of every three expectant women in the Western world are not living in the same community as their mother, grandmother, or biological sister. In other cultures, this would be rare. Do your best to find women who can be mentors, women you can look to as examples of stability and character. (Titus 2:4 says that the best way to learn how to love our families is from older, mature women of faith.) You and the women you value as spiritual "mothers" may not be able to enjoy long blocks of time together, but by watching their examples, you can grow in confidence as you look forward to the years of parenting ahead.

And don't forget that the women in the Bible have served as mentors for generations. Hebrews 11 clearly illustrates this. You can learn from mentors like Sarah, Abraham's wife.

Perhaps one of the most important steps of spiritual preparation for delivery, if you are far from your biological family, will be to find someone to act as a prayer partner and intercede for you throughout your pregnancy and labor. And you can look for the opportunity to be a prayer support for another expectant mother. In turning our eyes away from our own needs, we discover that unselfishness really is one of the keys of the kingdom of God.

Can I grow to spiritual maturity? you may have wondered. *Can I add to my personality the qualities of character that will make me a good mother?* The answer is *yes*. Yes, as you follow God's plan of growth! Spiritual growth is as natural as the growth of the embryo inside. God extends these promises to you as His daughter:

*Seek first the kingdom of God…and all
these things shall be added to you.*

MATTHEW 6:33

*Then we will no longer be infants…instead, speaking the
truth in love, we will in all things grow up into him.*

EPHESIANS 4:14-15 NIV

*F*aith *B*uilders

The Right Attitude

King David was a man after God's own heart. What was the attitude of David's heart that God found so pleasing? (See Psalm 42:1-2.)

_____

The apostle Paul also wrote of his constant spiritual hunger. Put Philippians 3:13-14 into your own words.

_____

_____

Do you need to increase your spiritual appetite? Pause right now to ask God to do a special work in your heart. Remember, "God is at work within you...helping you do what he wants" (Philippians 2:13 TLB).

The Right Action

We are given two tools with which to build up our spirits. First, we talk to God.

When do you have the privilege of praying?

1 Chronicles 16:11 _____

1 Thessalonians 5:17 _____

What is your attitude in prayer?

2 Chronicles 7:14 _____

Jeremiah 29:13 _____

Psalm 95:2 _____

What are we to do when we pray?

Mark 11:24 _____

James 1:6 _____

Second, we let God talk to us.

How do we gain more faith? (See Romans 10:17.)

_____

_____

What does the knowledge of God's Word bring about in our lives?
(See 2 Timothy 3:16-17 TLB.)

_____

The Bible deals with all aspects of life. Think about your own situation, and list several areas of life about which you would like the Lord to speak to you as you study His Word.

_____

_____

_____

James 1:21 says that the Word of God can be grafted or implanted into our lives. The original language uses the same word for impregnated!

The Word is like a tiny seed, full of life, that will grow naturally in our hearts.

The Right Relationship

Just as your physical body provides nourishment for the embryo within you, a church body will provide nourishment for the embryo of your spiritual experience. Study Romans 12:5-8 and list some of the ministries you will receive through consistent fellowship with other believers.

_____

_____

_____

What will a good church family add to your life? (See Jeremiah 3:15.)

_____

You are a busy woman in a busy society, and establishing a daily time of prayer and Bible study takes much discipline.

Set up a time. God walked with Adam and Eve each evening; David called on God each morning; Paul and Silas were good at praising God at midnight! What about you?

As you begin, set a realistic goal for yourself. (Reaching a small goal is better than becoming so discouraged that you give up completely.) Perhaps at first your daily devotions will include only five minutes of prayer and a chapter from the Word. But whatever goal you set, begin now! The habit should be well established before you enter the hectic period of caring for a newborn infant.

FURTHER DEVOTIONAL READING

I Can Be a Woman of Prayer

He spoke a parable to them, that men always ought to pray and not lose heart (Luke 18:1).

Also see Psalm 55:17; Daniel 6:10; Matthew 6:6; 26:41; Luke 11:9; Romans 8:26-27; 1 Corinthians 14:15

I Can Be a Woman of the Word

Your word was to me the joy and rejoicing of my heart (Jeremiah 15:16).

Also see Deuteronomy 8:3; 11:18; Job 23:12; Psalm 119:11,103; Colossians 3:16; 2 Timothy 3:16-17; 1 Peter 2:2; 2 Peter 1:21

I Can Be a Woman of Fellowship

Where two or three are gathered together in My name, I am there in the midst of them (Matthew 18:20).

Also see Psalm 111:1; 119:63; Malachi 3:16; Acts 2:42; Philippians 1:3,5; Hebrews 10:25; 1 John 1:7

$\mathcal{S}$UMMARY

Deep inside your uterus is a tiny but rapidly developing embryo. Within your body is another treasure that cannot be seen with the natural eye: your developing spirit. Both require watchful nutritional care.

As the child inside you and your spirit are both nourished during pregnancy, God's laws are set in motion. Growth is natural and inevitable. These months before delivery can add a quality to your life that will always remain with you.

$\mathcal{S}$arah, too, had faith, and because of this she was able to become a mother—in spite of her old age—for she realized that God, who gave her His promise, would certainly do what He had said.

HEBREWS 11:11 (TLB)

$\mathcal{L}$et GOD enlarge your families—giving growth to you, growth to your children.

PSALM 115:4 (MSG)

$\mathcal{H}$e who has begun a good work within you will complete it.

PHILIPPIANS 1:6

Things
My Doctor
Told Me This Month...

_____

_____

_____

_____

_____

_____

My Physical Changes...

_____

_____

_____

Things
I've Thought
About This Month...

_____

_____

_____

_____

_____

_____

My Special Verse...

_____

_____

_____

The Third Month

The fetus is now three inches long and weighs about an ounce. Hands and feet are fully formed; nails are distinctly present. Legs, arms, and fingers move spontaneously. External ears are evident. Eyelids are still fused. Tiny tooth sockets and buds are forming in jawbones. The ribs and backbone are soft and pliable. Heartbeat can now be detected with special instruments. Inside the brain, nerve cells are communicating with every part of the body.

Your baby may develop with head down or continue to rotate until the last weeks of pregnancy. It lives its uterine life within the "bag of waters," which serves as an excellent shock absorber. The amniotic fluid in this sack is not stagnant; it is completely replaced eight times each day.

You shall be happy

and it shall be well with you.

He has blessed your

children within you.

PSALM 128:2; 147:13

FREE FROM FEAR

*For God has not given us a spirit of fear, but
of power and of love and of a sound mind.*
2 TIMOTHY 1:7

Whenever I am afraid, I will trust in You.
PSALM 56:3

$\mathcal{B}$efore you were pregnant, you had no idea how much a developing baby would consume your thoughts. The new life inside you is your constant companion, not only in your body but also in your mind.

But suddenly, without warning, doubts and fears can invade your pleasant thoughts, turn your daydreams into nightmares, and rob you of the joy of pregnancy.

Obstetricians tell us that prenatal anxieties fall into three main categories: (1) fear of the disfigurement or miscarriage of the fetus, (2) fear of the pain involved in labor and delivery and the possible loss of your attractiveness following the birth, and (3) fear regarding the future safety and financial security of the child. By far the most prevalent is the first category—the fear that something may go wrong with the child within.

If we are not careful, worry can begin to control us. Worry if morning sickness sometimes keeps us from keeping down the pregnancy vitamins. Worry about the prescription medicines we took before we knew we were pregnant. Worry about a little spotting. Worry about that fall on the ice.

Each time you visit your obstetrician, you are given more tests than ever before. Your laboratory samples are screened for sugar and protein. You are weighed and prodded and asked a dozen questions. Even these wonderful precautions, which are meant to aid and comfort, can become a source of worry. One woman lamented, "After my visits to the doctor, I worry about conditions I hadn't even *heard* of before!"

Worry, according to one study, is the most common complaint of pregnancy, affecting more women than morning sickness and hunger cravings combined. In the widely read *What To Expect When You're Expecting,* author Heidi Murkoff says, "Ninety-four out of every one hundred women worry about whether their babies will be normal, and 93 percent worry that they and their babies will come through delivery safely."

At times you may wish your skin was transparent so you could look in and get just a glimpse of how your baby is doing. (If you could look inside your womb, you would see changes occurring almost daily, for at this time your baby's skin *is* almost transparent.) One frustrated woman even asked, "Why couldn't God have made human mothers the same way He made kangaroos, complete with a pouch on the outside where baby does most of its developing?"

The answer is that we could not resist attempting, however clumsily, to help the fetus along.

When we are afraid, we rush to "fix" the situation. Fear breeds manipulators. Psychologists tell us that controlling personalities, instead of being as strong as they appear, are actually motivated by fear. The way of the world is to manipulate, to contrive, to gain control in any way possible. But God's way is different.

He asks us to *trust*.

God is the only One who can knit together a new being. He couldn't allow us to get our hands on what must be His work and His alone. Your words to yourself must be the words of Psalm 62:5: "Wait silently for God alone."

You can dispel many fears about pregnancy, labor, and childbirth by obtaining accurate information. Instead of listening to the details of a neighbor's difficult delivery or to old wives' tales, ask your doctor questions, read available literature, and sign up now for a Prepared Childbirth class. (If you will not be accompanied in the labor room by your husband, Prepared Childbirth teachers will welcome a friend or your mother as your coach.) Now is the time to remember one of the most commonly quoted verses from the Bible: "The truth shall make you free" (John 8:32).

Momentary fear and concern is normal, for you are facing a brand-new experience. Your concerns are common to every woman who has ever carried a child. But what if your fears turn into giants that torment you? What is the source of tormenting fear?

The root of consuming fear is usually a mental or emotional lie, for psychological studies show us that many fears have no sound basis and focus on events that never take place. These lies are usually exaggerated thoughts or inaccurate pictures of the future. The Word of God tells us the source of these lies.

In 1 Peter 5:8 we see that, as God's children, we have an adversary, the devil. In John 8, Jesus describes Satan as the father of lies.

Your spiritual enemy endeavors to get you to accept lies and their resulting emotion—fear. Have you ever realized that you can accept or reject your thoughts? Have you realized that some of the ideas planted in your mind are not your own? You do not have to accept tormenting giants of fear!

And learning to reject fear is a scriptural practice that can bring incredible benefits, not just in pregnancy but for the rest of your life.

You are not defenseless! God offers you spiritual protection. You can *"put on all of God's armor so that you will be able to stand safe against all strategies and tricks of Satan"* (Ephesians 6:11 TLB).

In 2 Corinthians 10:5, we find two keys to mental stability: First, we are to cast down imaginations and mental speculations, and second, we are to take every thought captive under the lordship of Christ.

If fearful imaginations trouble you, determine to cast down these troubling thoughts from their place of influence over your emotions. When the apostle Paul wrote about "bringing every thought into captivity," the Greek word he used for *captivity* literally means "taken captive at sword point." In biblical times, people were arrested with swords held against their hearts. What a strong picture of how to control fear—Hebrews 4:12 explains that the sword of the Spirit is the Word of God!

"You will keep [her] in perfect peace, whose mind is stayed on you, because [she] trusts in You" (Isaiah 26:3). What expectant woman doesn't long for the days of gestation to be filled with peace? The peace of God will free you from fear. It will "guard your hearts and minds through Christ Jesus" (Philippians 4:7). In other words, the peace of God acts as a sentinel, standing guard at the gates of your mind. That peace can cushion your emotions and protect you just as surely as the amniotic fluid protects your baby!

You may have had an experience that concerned you, such as meeting a woman who has miscarried. Yet miscarriage in the early months is an act of grace in itself, for experts tell us that it is almost always the result of an improperly developed fetus. If the problem instead lies in a woman's physical makeup, the Lord can heal the miscarrying womb. Often, the Lord works through gifted physicians who have special wisdom for seeing a woman through a tentative pregnancy. (See Genesis 49:25 and the box on page 19-20.)

The truth is that this is the best of all possible times to be pregnant! Women enter pregnancy healthier than they used to, they get better prenatal care, and in the last decade, hospital maternity wings have been revolutionized, many equipped with NICUs (Newborn Intensive Care Units). Many medical and physical conditions that once threatened pregnancies have been overcome in the Western world.

Your baby is safer now, deep within the uterus, than it will ever be again! Pregnant women have been in auto accidents or have sustained bad falls, resulting in fractures of the limbs of their unborn babies. Yet those babies healed nicely in the womb without medical help and were born perfectly healthy! God has placed the fetus in a controlled, bacteria-free environment.

Soon the infant will grow to a toddler who faces the threat of contagious diseases, then to a child who faces playground cuts and bruises, then to a teenager who faces the strain of dating years, and then to a young adult who faces the challenge of independence. Sooner or later, unless you want to live as a nervous wreck, you must learn to be a mother who places her trust in God. By His grace you can learn *now*.

Yes, God does ask you to do your part. In a few short weeks you will be holding your baby, feeding it, caring for it constantly. But now is not the time. If the child you're carrying were able to speak to you at this time, he or she would whisper, "Mother, be at peace and let God knit me together. He knows what He is doing!"

$\mathcal{F}$AITH $\mathcal{B}$UILDERS

The Source of Fear

In John 8:32, Jesus promises us that we will find freedom by knowing the truth. One truth that the Scriptures emphasize time and time again is that God has an enemy, the devil. According to John 10:10, what three things does the devil endeavor to do?

_____

_____

Don't let your joy be stolen from you in what is supposed to be the most joyful time of life!

The Source of Serenity

We combat lies in the same way Jesus did when He confronted the devil in the wilderness. (See Luke 4.) We use God's Word. If you have been troubled by a recurring fear, search the Scriptures and find a verse to dispel that particular fear. (Your Bible concordance is the place to begin a word search, and an excellent free online concordance for all versions is available at www.biblegateway.com.) Write the verse here:

_____

_____

_____

Instead of allowing your mind to be filled with depressing fears, you can dwell on thoughts that will foster serenity. Read Philippians 4:8

and list the eight characteristics of the things we should think about.

_____

_____

_____

What attitude does 1 Timothy 4:7 say we should have about old wives' tales and superstition?

_____

_____

God provides His children with a suit of spiritual armor. Study Ephesians 6:14-17 and list the components of your protective covering.

_____

_____

_____

_____

_____

_____

Which of these applies most to your mind? Which applies most to your heart and emotions?

_____

Choosing Faith Instead of Fear

The Bible uses the example of a pregnant woman, Sarah, to define what faith really is!

> What is faith? It is the confident assurance that something we want is going to happen. It is the certainty that what we hope for is waiting for us, even though we cannot see it... Sarah, too, had faith, and because of this she was able to become a mother (Hebrews 11:1,11 TLB).

*F*URTHER *D*EVOTIONAL *R*EADING

God Will Watch Over My Delivery

Blessed shall be the fruit of your body (Deuteronomy 28:4).

Also see Deuteronomy 7:13-15; 28:1-11

I Can Follow These Examples of Faith and Fearlessness

By faith Sarah herself also received strength to conceive seed, and she bore a child when she was past the age, because she judged Him faithful who had promised (Hebrews 11:11).

Also read about Sarah in Genesis 17:15-16, Esther in Esther 4:14-16, and Hannah in 1 Samuel 1–2.

I Have Authority over God's Enemy

Therefore submit to God. Resist the devil and he will flee from you (James 4:7).

Zechariah 3:2; Luke 10:17-19; 22:31-32; John 12:31; Acts 5:16; Ephesians 4:26-27; 6:11-12; Hebrews 2:14; 1 John 3:8

I Don't Have to Be Afraid

Do not be afraid, Zacharias, for your prayer is heard; and your wife Elizabeth will bear you a son…and you will have joy and gladness" (Luke 1:13-14).

Also see Matthew 14:30-31; 17:6-7; Mark 4:38-40; 5:33-34; 16:5-6; John 20:19

Examples of needless fear. Matthew 14:30; 17:6; Mark 4:38; 5:33; 16:5

SUMMARY

You cannot yet see the child developing inside you. The Lord cannot allow us to manipulate something as fragile as the fetus, so in His wisdom, He seals the baby deep within the mother's uterus. According to the verses we have studied above, this is exactly the time to be a woman of faith!

"Don't worry about anything; instead, pray about everything" (Philippians 4:6 TLB). Believe that every tiny part of your baby-to-be is being fashioned by a wise heavenly Father, for *faith* brings *freedom from fear.*

Things
My Doctor
Told Me This Month...

_____

_____

_____

_____

_____

_____

My Physical Changes...

_____

_____

_____

Things
I've Thought
About This Month . . .

_____

_____

_____

_____

_____

My Special Verse . . .

_____

_____

_____

The Fourth Month

Your baby is now six and one-half to seven inches long and weighs five ounces. The heartbeat is strong and can be easily detected by a physician. Muscles are developed and active, and the lower parts of the body show rapid growth. Skin is bright pink and wrinkled. Eyes, ears, nose, and mouth approach typical appearance.

The uterus begins to enlarge noticeably with the developing fetus and can now be felt extending halfway up to the umbilicus.

You made all the delicate, inner parts
of my body and knit them together in
my mother's womb. Thank you for
making me so wonderfully complex!
It is amazing to think about. Your
workmanship is marvelous—
and how well I know it.

PSALM 139:13-14 (TLB)

A STUDY IN STABILITY

He will feed his flock like a shepherd;
He will gather the lambs with His arm,
and carry them in His bosom, and shall
gently lead those who are with young.

ISAIAH 40:11

Through the miraculous process God has woven into His laws of nature, your body is undergoing tremendous change in order to nourish the child inside it.

Special hormones are filling your bloodstream with an entirely new chemistry. The amount of some of the hormones in your system, such as crucially important estrogen, will more than *triple* before the baby is born. Your entire metabolism is readjusting; your body fluid and blood volume increase, your blood pressure increases, and your heartbeat will even quicken.

Perhaps you have read that these physical changes often bring emotional side effects. Friends have told you how touchy they were during pregnancy. "I burst into tears for the slightest reason," they confess. "My life was a string of emotional highs and lows for the entire nine months." Or maybe you have noticed how sentimental you feel; you can no longer watch the evening news with your husband without feeling upset, and a Hallmark commercial can move you to tears!

This is a perfect month to begin to practice better self-discipline about allowing certain influences into your life. If you struggle with some hormonal depression, turn down that tear-jerker movie and opt for a comedy. If the detective drama you used to find interesting now disturbs you, go to bed early with a cup of milk and a soothing book.

You are coping with six noticeable areas of change:

1. cessation of menses
2. breast and abdominal enlargement
3. energy depletion
4. digestive problems such as heartburn, constipation, or nausea
5. pressure on bones and stretching of tendons
6. surges in hormone levels and possible fluctuations in the sexual drive

These changes can be tremendously upsetting if you allow them to be, placing you on an emotional roller coaster and taking your loved ones along for the tearfully turbulent ride.

You may not always understand the things you are feeling. But medical experts assure us that *all* women have both positive and negative attitudes toward pregnancy. *All* women have both positive and negative attitudes about motherhood. Realize that the negative thoughts are not aimed at the baby but rather at *your condition and lifestyle changes.*

You may go through stages of feeling depressingly unattractive. Combine a few flattering maternity outfits with interchangeable accessories. Try a new hairstyle, weekly facials, a soak in a scented tub, and one of the skin creams especially made for pregnancy. Most of all, remember to let your *inner radiance shine through.* The radiance that God has built into pregnancy will more than make up for your changing figure!

You are in a new season. Every season in the natural world brings its own unique reward: the warm days and flowers of spring, the carefree heat and harvest of late summer, the crisp wind and glorious leaves of autumn, the sparkling snow and holidays of winter. You are in a special season—one that men will never experience, one that some women never get to know, one that will cover only a few of the months in the years of your lifetime. And just as in every season, God offers you unique rewards.

Psalm 1:3 promises that you can be like a tree planted by streams of water, having fruit in every season. Your leaves will not wither, and everything you do will prosper.

Sociologists have identified several stages of adult emotional development. A woman's season for childbearing is called *rooting and extending,* and old-fashioned books even call it the season of *nesting.* Your heart is wanting to prepare a safe nest for a new generation. Enjoy it!

But the same sociologists have identified one possible pitfall for women in this stage, and that is the tendency to be turned too inward or become myopic.

Spending a lot of time thinking about yourself and the development of the baby is normal. Yet be cautious that introversion doesn't cause you to withdraw from your husband or those around you. Don't be so preoccupied with your own needs that you forget his. Embrace your husband emotionally just as you will soon embrace your infant. Let him in on what you are thinking; don't expect him to be telepathic! He is very concerned about you and about the baby, but he may show it in different ways. For example, he may work longer hours to bring in needed income. By the way, physicians agree that normal sexual intimacy can continue until the final six weeks of pregnancy unless you experience physical discomfort (see 1 Corinthians 7:5).

The Word of God has much to say about each situation we may face in life—even pregnancy. Is getting up each day difficult for you because of morning sickness? "When I awake, I will be satisfied with seeing your likeness" (Psalm 17:15 NIV). Do you feel drained of energy? "He gives power to the weak, and to those who have no might he increases strength...Those who wait on the LORD shall renew their strength" (Isaiah 40:29,31). Do you need God to touch you physically because of nagging back or leg aches? "I am the LORD who heals you" (Exodus 15:26). "You can get anything—anything you ask for in prayer—if you believe" (Matthew 21:22 TLB).

Remember at all times during your pregnancy that God understands you and looks at you tenderly. When you feel emotionally shaky, never be ashamed to turn to Him. "He is like a father to us, tender and sympathetic to those who reverence him. For he knows we are but dust" (Psalm 103:13-14 TLB). He is our Good Shepherd, and remember that Isaiah 40:11 tells us He will "gently lead those who are with young."

When we yearn for emotional stability, we must remember that our spirit and soul are so woven into our bodies that emotional health and physical health cannot be separated. We can lose emotional battles and even spiritual battles because our physical resistance is low. In the first months of pregnancy you feel the need for extra rest. Don't fight fatigue! Your body is busy, creating an entirely new person! Climb into bed for a short nap if you can, or if you are at work, at least put your feet up and relax.

One day, when your child becomes a toddler, you will see that whining or tears and yawning every afternoon can only mean one thing: nap time! You will have compassion for that little one and be very understanding of his or her needs. David saw that our heavenly Father looks at us with the same parental tenderness: "You chart the path ahead of me and tell me where to stop and rest" (Psalm 139:3 TLB). How amazing to see the Lord in that way, as One who even cares if you get enough rest. This is an excellent time to open your Bible and receive the soothing ministry of God's Word as you see His concern for even the small details of your life.

Chapter 5 will deal further with the care of your body, for being in top physical condition as you face childbirth and motherhood is crucial. But to discipline your body, you must learn to discipline your mind. The disciplined mind produces emotional stability.

Remember what you studied earlier about the source of tormenting fear? You can choose to accept or reject the thoughts of fear that your spiritual enemy whispers to you. The same is true with other thoughts! Thoughts of self-pity. Thoughts of resentment. Thoughts of frustration or anger.

As you grew up, you settled into certain thought patterns. You may have never realized the importance of disciplining your mind, and so you may spend a lot of time entertaining thoughts that harm your emotional stability. All through school in P.E. classes, and as adults at every gym and health club, we are reminded of the importance of discipline for the body. Yet in Western cultures, we seldom talk about mental discipline. In Philippians 4:7-8 God gives a better alternative to letting our minds wander aimlessly. And 1 Peter 1:13

tells us, "Gird up [get control of]...your mind." Many believers have never realized how many verses of Scripture are promises that the Creator wants to help us regain our self-control!

This month in your pregnancy is a good time to meditate on the fruit of the Holy Spirit listed in Galatians 5:22: "The fruit of the Spirit is love, joy, peace, patience, kindness, goodness, faithfulness, gentleness and self-control" (NIV).

We have two ways to live. We can live at the mercy of the situation in which we find ourselves, ruled by fluctuating emotions, or as God's daughters, we can begin to reign in life!

> All who will take God's gift of forgiveness and acquittal
> are kings [and queens] of life because of this one man,
> Jesus Christ (Romans 5:17 TLB).

Think of it! A queen of *life!* Not a rollercoaster rider, not an emotional wreck, but a woman of inner strength and stability who can enjoy the precious season of her pregnancy.

$\mathcal{F}$AITH $\mathcal{B}$UILDERS

The Reason Behind the Warning

According to Proverbs 23:7, what is the outward result of your inner thought life?

_____

Your imagination is God given, but excessive daydreaming can lead to discontent and restlessness. How does the Bible tell us to handle our thoughts? (See Jeremiah 4:14.)

_____

In Matthew 15:18-20 Jesus warns about destructive thinking and lists several main categories of destructive thoughts. What are they?

_____

Can you think of subtle thoughts that would fit in each of those major categories?

Steps Toward Discipline

Repentance always helps free us from old habits. What action are we asked to take in 2 Corinthians 4:2?

_____

What do these verses teach us to do when our mind wanders?

Ephesians 4:17 _____

2 Corinthians 10:5b _____

According to James 1:8, what is one of the major causes of emotional instability?

_____

Are you facing a decision that has not yet been resolved? Ask your Father to guide you in making this decision.

The Positive Provision
How can a woman who feels a little shaky emotionally experience transformation?

    Ephesians 4:22-24 _____

    Romans 12:1-2 _____

Through the power of the Holy Spirit, what can take the place of our undisciplined thought life? (See 1 Corinthians 2:16.)

_____

You will keep [her] in perfect peace,
Whose mind is stayed on You,
Because [she] trusts in You.

ISAIAH 26:3

Further Devotional Reading

I Can Have a Disciplined Mind

> Do not be conformed to this world, but be transformed by the renewing of your mind, that you may prove what is that good and acceptable and perfect will of God (Romans 12:2).

Also see Proverbs 4:23; 22:11; Jeremiah 4:14; Luke 6:45; Ephesians 4:17,22-23

I Can Control My Emotions

> [Bring] every thought into captivity to the obedience of Christ (2 Corinthians 10:5).

Also see Proverbs 16:32; Romans 6:12; 1 Corinthians 9:27; 2 Peter 1:5-7

ᏚUMMARY

Perhaps you have never before realized that the Lord wants you to be a queen of life! In 2 Corinthians 4:7 you are promised that through the power of God you can learn to reign!

The woman who can reign over her own thought life will be able to reign over her emotions. This month's priority is a disciplined mind!

In quietness and in confidence
shall be your strength.

ISAIAH 30:15

Wisdom and knowledge will be
the stability of your times.

ISAIAH 33:6

Things
My Doctor
Told Me This Month...

_____

_____

_____

_____

_____

_____

My Physical Changes...

_____

_____

_____

Things
I've Thought
About This Month...

_____

_____

_____

_____

_____

_____

My Special Verse...

_____

_____

_____

The Fifth Month

Your baby is from seven to ten inches long and weighs from eight to ten ounces. Internal organs are maturing at astonishing speed. A covering like peach fuzz appears over the entire body. At the end of the month, hair begins to grow on the baby's scalp. The baby's senses continue to awaken; in addition to hearing the sounds of mother's blood and heartbeat, he may even discern her voice. The reflex for nursing is already beginning—if baby's hand drifts near his mouth, he may suck his thumb! Baby's movements do more than exercise growing limbs— the sensations from moving about help establish nerve connections and pathways in the brain that will be used after birth. If your baby is a boy, he is already producing the hormone testosterone. If your baby is a girl, eggs are starting to develop in her tiny ovaries.

But the very hairs of your

head are all numbered.

MATTHEW 10:30

Thus says the Lord, your

Redeemer, and He who formed

you from the womb; "I am the

Lord, who makes all things."

ISAIAH 44:24

IN CONTROL

A [person] without self-control is as
defenseless as a city with broken-down walls.

*Y*our responsibility toward your developing fetus is to provide it with a healthy environment. To do this, you must maintain constant vigilance toward your own health.

Like most women, you probably left the medical professional's office following your first pregnancy exam armed with booklets on good nutrition, a prescription for prenatal vitamins, and the strong determination to get proper foods, plenty of rest, and daily exercise. At first it sounded like fun! Yet now that several months have elapsed, steak and salad may have given way to pizza and Cokes, the "daily" vitamins may be remembered a few times a week, and when it comes to exercise, you probably tell yourself, *I'll take a long walk tomorrow...*

Are you well disciplined? Are you disgustingly undisciplined? Or, like most of us, are you out of control, then in control, and then disappointingly out again?

Building Up the Walls

Proverbs 25:28 compares a person lacking self-discipline to an Old Testament city without the security of strong outer walls. In those times and up through the Middle Ages, the doom of an unprotected city was certain. And even in the twenty-first century, the walls of great cities such as York in England, Carcassonne in France, and Dubrovnik in Croatia have survived. In the symbolism of the Bible, a woman who is out of control has no walls of protection and will be the target of attack in mind, in soul, and in body. In the previous chapter we talked about being a queen who learns to reign in life. This month, meditate on what the Word has to say about reigning over our bodies.

In the sixth century BC, Babylonians conquered Jerusalem and tore down its mighty walls. Under the leadership of Nehemiah, 142 years later, some Jews returned from Babylon to their beloved Jerusalem. What was their mission? "Come and let us build up the wall of Jerusalem, that we may no longer be a reproach" (Nehemiah 2:17). The Israelites knew that without the city walls to protect them, they would be at the mercy of surrounding hostile tribes.

Jerusalem is the city of which God said, "Sing praises to the LORD, who dwells in Zion!" (Psalm 9:11). After the coming of Christ, through the power of the Holy Spirit, God promises to actually dwell in the hearts of His children. "I will dwell in them and walk in them; and I will be their God, and they shall be My people" (2 Corinthians 6:16). As a dwelling place of the Lord, Jerusalem is actually a picture, an illustration, a symbolic example of the life of a Christian. Just as God's will was to protect Zion with fortified walls, God wants to help you build up walls of self-control in your life.

Self-Control

You may feel that your "walls" are a hopeless rubble. Perhaps you have been lacking in discipline all your life, and this lack has only been magnified by your condition. (The unique craving for certain foods that occurs in pregnancy has its own name: *pica.*) You may have struggled with a weight problem, or with doing your house-work and necessary chores, or with the myriad of responsibilities that come your way. You may be thinking, *Certain areas of my life have gotten away from me, and I want to get them in control—but my motivational powers are zilch!* Like the apostle Paul, you cry, "I don't understand myself at all, for I really want to do what is right, but I can't!" (Romans 7:15 TLB).

But Paul found the answer, and you can too. He asked, "Who will free me from my slavery to this lower deadly nature?" Then he recorded the answer: "Thank God! It has been done by Jesus Christ our Lord" (Romans 7:24-25 TLB).

You see, Jesus didn't just tell us how to live and then give us a farewell pat on the back and say, "Lots of luck!" He didn't leave us to struggle along on our own. He promised an unlimited, ever-available power source: The Holy Spirit.

Ephesians 6:10 tells us that because of the Holy Spirit, we can "Be strong in the Lord and in the power of His might." The Greek word translated *strong* means "infused with great inner strength." (*Dunamao* is the root of our word *dynamo!*)

Through the miraculous indwelling of the Holy Spirit, your pregnancy and your entire life can be as secure as a fortified city. Building on the foundation of the Rock of Jesus Christ, the Spirit will patiently rebuild your willpower. Allow Him to add divine force to the strength of your own determination, for—and this is a very sobering thought—when our physical desire is out of control, it actually becomes a god that we worship. Paul describes people in this situation in Philippians 3:19—"Their god is their appetite."

When we are at the mercy of our desires and cravings, we are out of control. God wants you to be in control and able to...

- ∾ maintain your proper weight
- ∾ care for your body and your developing child through rest and exercise
- ∾ accomplish all of those things a woman in waiting needs to accomplish

In the previous chapter, we focused on disciplining your mind according to God's Word. Now you are ready for steps of outward discipline. Just as Romans 5:17 applies to ruling as a queen over your mind, you can also exercise *bodily control* as you reign in life!

This month is the time when, if you have not already, you will feel the movements of the little life inside you. In Old Testament or Jewish terminology, this is called *quickening* (in Hebrew, *cha-yah*—"to be full of life"). The growing recognition of that life within you can help you build up your self-control. These gentle pokes and fluttering taps from your baby make the discomforts of pregnancy worthwhile. The feel of this new life inspires you to grow in self-discipline and improve your physical health. The "protecting walls" of self-control around your own life will also protect your baby!

Yes and No

Self-control includes two components: the ability to say *no* to some things, and the ability to say *yes* to others.

We learn to say *no* to things that would harm the fetus, including alcohol, pain killers, and tempting but too-salty food (if high blood pressure becomes a concern—high blood pressure that can lead to toxemia in pregnancy).

We learn to say *yes* to things that will help the baby grow. Fitness during pregnancy means more than just staying active. It includes deep breathing, proper posture, and stretching and relaxation. The American College of Obstetricians and Gynecologists recommends moderate exercise for at least 30 minutes every day provided your own doctor approves. Keeping fit can actually help you to avoid much of the back pain that plagues many mothers to be. It will increase your stamina in labor and even speed your recovery after delivery.

Recent clinical studies have shown that your baby also benefits when you improve your fitness. Regular exercise by a mother to be can strengthen the placenta, help the baby tolerate labor's contractions, and maybe even enhance the physical and mental abilities of the infant! And swimming classes or other fitness classes for pregnant women can also lead to lasting new friendships and the emotional support system that new moms need.

Self-control is saying yes to your physician's advice. More medical tests are given now in the fifth month than were available before. For example, this month your doctor will probably want to run a test for hepatitis B. This is because hepatitis B, unlike the old hepatitis A, can be passed on to the fetus, and if you have been exposed, your baby can be treated at birth so that the infection can't continue. Say yes to the prescription vitamins even though they look like horse pills! Say yes to admonitions about careful dental care; your gums may tend to bleed as the fetus takes more minerals from your system.

As you grow in self-control, you will be able to accomplish more. As children, we are often procrastinators, but as adults, we must grow up in our attitude toward responsibility. You have a nursery to prepare and a layette to ready—and maybe furniture to purchase and closets to rearrange. If you have a demanding job, you have projects to finish before your maternity leave. Soon, as a new mother, your tasks may seem overwhelming. But this is where personal growth in self-control will be a blessing. Maturity is a time to face the things you need to accomplish and to ask God's help when setting priorities.

Perfectionism

Some women are not procrastinators but instead fall at the other end of the personality spectrum. These women might call themselves workaholics—they cannot stand to leave a job undone. If you fit into this category, you will need self-control to accept the new limitations of energy and stamina that pregnancy places on your body. Pay careful attention to your body's signals. If you become breathless when exercising or feel as if the vacuum suddenly weighs a ton, take a break. Self-control is *not* perfectionism. We do not need to look like the pregnant model on the cover of *Parenting* magazine, and we do not need to prepare a nursery that looks like something in *Better Homes and Gardens!* Remember that all advertising is a *mirage.* Say no to the terrible burden of being a perfectionist.

Romans 8:37 says that "in all these things" (and that includes the things we face daily in our journey to motherhood) "we are more than conquerors through Him who loved us." It is another way of wording the promise in Romans 5:17—we can learn to "reign in life through the One, Jesus Christ."

ℱAITH ℬUILDERS

A Biblical Perspective

According to Proverbs 16:32, what is the value placed on self-control?

_____

The Bible sometimes uses the word *discipline* when speaking of self-control and teaches that discipline determines what kind of woman you become (see Proverbs 4:23). What are two of the benefits of self-control?

Proverbs 12:24 _____

Proverbs 10:4; 21:5 _____

How does Proverbs 23:21 describe an undisciplined person? How does this apply to the woman in waiting?

_____

In Isaiah 37:3, how does Hezekiah describe the "day of trouble"?

_____

A Biblical Picture

The rebuilding of Jerusalem serves as an illustration of rebuilding areas of our lives. According to Zechariah 4:7, how were the people to accomplish this monumental task?

_____

To understand Zechariah 4:7 we need a clear definition of the word *grace*. Grace is the working of God through His mercy. According to 2 Corinthians 12:9, what are perfect opportunities for God to show His strengthening grace?

_____

How can God's power help us control the desires of our bodies? (See Romans 8:13.)

_____

Personal Application

Read about the special fruit of the Spirit that is listed in Galatians 5:22-23.

Part of the fruit of the Spirit is gentleness or meekness. The original word did not mean humbleness as we might suppose. The Greek word actually refers to *a strong will that is brought under control*. It was used to describe wild animals that had been tamed, such as a powerful stallion that was trained to pull a chariot.

The final fruit on the list is self-control. This refers to power over one's passions, appetites, and desires. In what area of your life do you need the Spirit to help you with self-control?

_____

If you have not already memorized the fruit of the Spirit as listed in Galatians 5:22-23, now would be the perfect time to do so.

As in all areas of spiritual growth, self-control will develop gradually, not all at once. What encouragement to engage the process does 1 Corinthians 9:25 offer?

_____

_____

As we saw in this chapter, when an area of our life is out of control, it becomes a god. What does Isaiah 26:13 promise about our personal freedom? (See the New International Version or Living Bible paraphrase.)

_____

FURTHER DEVOTIONAL READING

God Cares About My Diet

> Whether you eat or drink, or whatever you do, do all
> to the glory of God (1 Corinthians 10:31).

Also see Psalm 141:4; Proverbs 23:1,2,20; 25:16,27; Isaiah 55:2; Luke 10:8; 12:22-24; 21:34; Romans 14:21; 1 Corinthians 10:25; 1 Timothy 4:4-5

God Will Give Me Rest

> Come to Me, all you who labor and are heavy laden,
> and I will give you rest (Matthew 11:28).

Also see Isaiah 28:12; Jeremiah 30:17; Zephaniah 3:17

I Can Be in Control

> Therefore, as the elect of God, holy and beloved, put
> on tender mercies, kindness, humility, meekness, patience
> (see Colossians 3:12-13).

Also see Romans 6:6; 13:13-14; 1 Corinthians 9:25-27; Galatians 5:16; Colossians 3:5; Titus 2:1-5; 1 Peter 2:11; 3:10-11; 4:1-2

God Is My Source of Power

> I will put My Spirit within you and cause you to walk
> in My statutes, and you will keep My ways and do them
> (see Ezekiel 36:27).

Also see Matthew 3:11; Luke 11:13; John 15:5; Acts 1:8; 2:38; Romans 8:11; 1 Corinthians 3:16

$\mathcal{S}$UMMARY

People are more susceptible to certain illnesses when their resistance is low. Self-discipline protects your health from the physical problems that can attack when you lack adequate exercise, rest, and nutrition. It also protects you from the mental and emotional assaults we have discussed in previous chapters.

How will we be able to discipline our children if we have not learned to discipline ourselves? This month's priority is control over your body! With God's help, you are able!

$\mathcal{B}$ut we have this treasure in earthen vessels,
that the excellence of the power
may be of God and not of us.

2 CORINTHIANS 4:7

Things
My Doctor
Told Me This Month...

_____

_____

_____

_____

_____

_____

_____

My Physical Changes...

_____

_____

_____

Things
I've Thought
About This Month . . .

_____

_____

_____

_____

_____

_____

My Special Verse . . .

_____

_____

_____

The Sixth Month

Your baby has now grown to be ten to fourteen inches long and weighs two pounds. The muscles are more active, and because of the baby's size, you often feel movement! Nails form on the tiny fingers and toes. At the end of the month, eyelids are separated, and eyes are fully formed.

You are worthy, O Lord, to receive

glory and honor and power;

for You created all things,

and by Your will they exist

and were created.

REVELATION 4:11

THE GIFT OF SIGHT

We know about these things because God has
sent his Spirit to tell us, and his Spirit searches
out and shows us all of God's deepest secrets…
The spiritual man has insight into everything.

1 CORINTHIANS 2:10,15 TLB

*T*he womb is neither dark nor silent.

During this sixth month, the developing baby's previously fused eyelids are finally separated. Although bright light doesn't penetrate the uterus, the baby's eyes do begin to open and shut, and he or she is able to see!

At the same time, your baby is acquiring a sense of hearing. The sounds range from the rhythm of your heartbeat and the sound of your voice to the crash and vibration of outside street noises. Expectant mothers often notice that their baby may prefer a certain type of music. Scripture gives an example of an unborn child reacting to an outside voice. When Elizabeth, who was pregnant with John the Baptist, heard the voice of the expectant Mary, she said the babe in her womb leaped for joy! (See Luke 1:44.)

How rapidly the baby has developed from an embryo to a fetus with amazing abilities! Just as your unborn infant is acquiring perceptive ability, you can be acquiring spiritual perception and insight.

Spiritual Insight

Many women do not realize that the spiritual dimension is every bit as real as the physical dimension of life. In fact, the spiritual dimension is more real—it existed before the physical world and will remain after this world has ended. Many rely solely on their natural abilities, such as sight and hearing. As a woman who has a relationship with the living God and is receiving spiritual nourishment (as we studied earlier), you can become more sensitive to the unseen dimension.

Our society, which operates outside of the principles of God, presses in on us with its ungodly way of living. The Bible refers to the unbeliever as the "natural man" and says this:

> The man who isn't a Christian can't understand and can't accept these thoughts from God, which the Holy Spirit teaches us (1 Corinthians 2:14 TLB).

This is why Romans 12:2 (PHILLIPS) gives us this warning:

> Don't let the world around you squeeze you into its own mould, but let God re-make you so that your whole attitude of mind is changed. Thus you will prove in practice that the plan of God for you is good.

This sixth month of pregnancy brings great excitement. Your baby has been moving before, but now your loved ones can see the movements of the new life! In the previous chapter, we saw that the Hebrews called this *quickening*. During this time, God can "quicken" your understanding to new spiritual insights. Scriptural concepts that have seemed to be only tradition or mere words can leap to life! And the growth of your spiritual life will be obvious to friends and family.

What are some of these principles of growth that are especially meaningful to the woman in waiting?

Positive Confession

Earlier, we looked at verses from God's Word about emotional stability. Your spiritual exercise was to discipline your mind and stand against tormenting fear or worry or other negative emotions. You discovered the principle of filling your mind with "Whatever things are true." Now it is time to take another step of spiritual maturity: speaking by faith.

This spiritual insight will show you a way of living that greatly differs from the way of the world. The world would mold you into a woman who speaks negatively. Have you heard yourself say, "I'll probably be just like my mom and have an unusually long labor"? With the psalmist, the woman in waiting needs to pray, "Set a guard, O Lord, over my mouth" (Psalm 141:3).

Jesus said that "by your words you will be justified, and by your words you will be condemned" (Matthew 12:37). In Mark 11:23, He dealt further with the principle of positive confession: "He will have whatever he says."

In 1 Timothy 5:13, Paul warned that one quality of foolish women is that they are "saying things which they ought not." You can learn to be a wise woman, with the spiritual insight to speak with *faith* about the birth of your baby

- ✺ I'm looking forward to the birth of my baby.
- ✺ I know God promises to be with me continually, and so I am not afraid.
- ✺ I know God will bless me with calmness and strength.
- ✺ I believe He will help me to be a good mother.

This is not just positive thinking. It is the scriptural principle of verbally affirming God's promises. Remember, "the word [of faith] is near you, in your mouth" (Romans 10:8).

The Power of Praise

Open your spiritual ears to hear what the Holy Spirit wants to teach you about the exercise of praise.

Is *praise* a word that you associate only with the Thanksgiving holiday or Handel's "Hallelujah Chorus"? If the idea of praise seems foreign to you, if your only involvement in praise has been as a part of formal church liturgy, the Bible can open your eyes to an entirely new way to live.

To praise God means to speak or sing your thankfulness. Praise can flow from your heart during your devotional time, as you do your housework...anytime! This exercise is similar to physical exercise—you may not feel like doing it until you actually begin. But with practice, praise will become a well-developed spiritual response.

1. Praise God for *who He is*. "O Lord, you are worthy to receive the glory and the honor and the power" (Revelation 4:11 TLB). This lifts you out of the trap of too much introspection. Physicians tell us that our bodies operate

more smoothly if we don't concentrate on every minute twinge or small pain.

2. Praise God for *what He has done.* Revelation 4:11 continues, "You have created all things. They were created and called into being by your act of will." Thank Him for the conception of your child. Thank Him for your spiritual growth in the past weeks and in the weeks ahead.

3. Praise God for *what He will do.* Hannah and Elizabeth, along with other women of faith whose stories are recorded in the Bible, thanked God for their children before they were born. Psalm 22:3 teaches us that God inhabits, or lives in, the praises of His people! The woman who learns to praise experiences a special awareness of God's presence.

Communion

Many of us have received the Lord's Supper regularly since childhood. This month, allow your Father to open your eyes to a new understanding of communion, for this powerful symbol of Christ's death and resurrection is especially meaningful to the woman in waiting and her developing child.

> For every time you eat this bread and drink this cup, you are representing and signifying and proclaiming the fact of the Lord's death [and resurrection] until he comes [again] (1 Corinthians 11:26 AMP).

The true meaning of communion is the proclamation of the resurrection power! When received with understanding, it can be a dynamic instrument of physical and emotional health for the believer. First Corinthians 11:30 even goes so far as to tell us that some early

Christians suffered weakness and illness because they didn't perceive the tremendous significance of communion.

Think of this truth as it applies to your baby. You are already well aware that everything that enters your system travels through the placenta and into the child's system. This is why a balanced diet is so crucial and why you must be cautious of even the mildest medication. When you receive the bread and juice of communion, some of the digested molecules literally become a part of the baby, proclaiming the fact of the Lord's resurrection power, the fact of His wholeness, to the body of the little one!

For the woman who bears a new life within her, the celebration of communion becomes much more than ceremony or tradition. In a very tangible way, you are sharing your faith in the reality of God's love with the little one growing inside you.

The Gift of Discernment

In the Bible, the ability to see and hear in the Spirit is called *discernment.* Discernment is the quality that enables us to see things as God sees them. God-given discernment will enable you to see a situation as it really is so that you can deal with the root of a problem instead of only its symptoms.

A lovely young woman named Celia said, "I don't want my husband to go through delivery with me because Don is the nervous type, and I'm sure he wouldn't make it." One day during devotions, Celia discerned what was really in her heart and realized that she was afraid she might take the stress of labor out on her husband, snapping at him and perhaps ruining the joy of their teamwork. As the couple discussed her fear, her husband reassured her of his understanding love regardless of her reaction to the strain of labor. They held hands and prayed about it. When the time of her delivery arrived, Celia and Don worked together as a perfect unit during the birth of their baby girl.

Another young woman named Sarah often worried out loud in her pregnancy, "I just wasn't ready to become pregnant." One day as she was thinking about spiritual priorities and her desire to buy a home instead of rent, she realized that the material blessing of owning a home would not make her a better mother. Godly wisdom and discernment will keep the world around you from squeezing you into its mold. As motherhood approaches, let the Lord be the One who dictates your lifestyle. See things *His* way, not man's way, in such areas as how to build your marriage, how to discipline your children, and how many material possessions you really need.

Jesus said the Holy Spirit is our Teacher. "But I will send you the Comforter—the Holy Spirit, the source of all truth. He will come to you from the Father and will tell you all about me" (John 15:26 TLB). The Spirit hears us as we ask Him to be our Teacher.

*Open my eyes to see
wonderful things in your Word.*

PSALM 119:18 TLB

Seeing Through Ultrasound

Sometime around your twentieth week of pregnancy, your physician will probably schedule an appointment for an ultrasound—a technique that uses high-frequency sound waves for imaging. This miracle of modern medical technology was unimaginable to women of the past, and just a few years ago, it was only offered when physicians had reason to be concerned about the fetus. Today, some insurance programs even allow for several different ultrasounds during your nine months of waiting.

In your sixth month of pregnancy, an ultrasound will usually show a technician the sex of your baby! Some couples choose not to know; other times the baby simply refuses to cooperate and turns in such a way that the images are not clear. But for many women, this is the moment when you will know for sure that you are having a daughter or a son.

The revelation often brings a mix of interesting feelings. Perhaps you were raised in a family of all girls, and you're stunned to hear you're having a boy. Perhaps you already have two beautiful daughters, and find out you're carrying another girl. Maybe you even received the shocking news that you have two strong little boys in your womb, and you are feeling anything but strong enough for twins. Whatever announcement you receive, the day always is filled with contemplation.

It is a moment we have in common with Mary, the mother of Jesus. When she was given information about her little boy, Luke 2:51 (TLB) says she "stored away all these things in her heart"—she contemplated them deeply.

A few other Bible women received information about the children they were carrying. For example, in Genesis 25:22, Rebekah was having such a painful pregnancy that she asked God "If all is well, why am I like this?" The Lord revealed to her that she was having twins; the struggle within her would produce two men who would found two different nations! But as a rule, women of the past had no foreknowledge, no time to know what colors to plan for the baby's room or to prepare their hearts for exactly who was coming!

The timing of a conception and the sex of each fetus is something that is still completely in God's hands. Even women who have struggled through fertility treatment and medicine know with certainty that life itself can only come from God. We can pray with confidence, *You knew this child before it was even conceived!* (see Psalm 139:16). Your child is a part of God's great plan, whether male or female.

In Jewish culture, each new baby boy will be welcomed with a *Shalom Zachar* and a *Bris Milah*. He will be named and welcomed into the covenant. As in the Old Testament, a boy is viewed as the fulfillment of a promise and a necessity (as an heir and the one who will carry on the traditions). In Jewish culture, growing numbers of parents celebrate *Simchat Bat* (the naming and "joy of a daughter.") In Aramaic, the phrase is *zeved bat*, inspired by Abraham's experience (see Genesis 24:1). The parents say, "God gave me the fullness of everything"—that is, the fulfillment of joy in the birth of a daughter from whom future generations of faith will come.

Boy or girl, the child growing within you is a treasure of infinite value. "In Christ's family...you are all equal" (Galatians 3:28 MSG). The Lord will equip you to be the parent that this unique being will need.

ℱaith ℬuilders

God-Given Insight

How does 1 Corinthians 1:25 compare our natural wisdom with the wisdom of God?

How does James 4:17 describe God-given wisdom?

According to James 1:5, how can we obtain godly wisdom?

What will be the result of your receptive (teachable) attitude? (See James 3:18.)

Read Psalm 119:18. What is the reason for the special "sight" mentioned in this verse?

Spiritual "Quickening"

Study Mark 11:23-24 and write a statement of faith about your unborn child.

Praise is a powerful spiritual practice. What concept from Psalm 100:4 can you add to your daily prayer times?

_____

We learn to praise not only by feeling but also by faith (see Psalm 107:22). Are you learning, like David, to say "I will bless the LORD at all times" (Psalm 34:1)?

_____

According to Matthew 26:26,28, what do the two elements of the communion service represent?

_____

What powerful message is proclaimed by this twofold ceremony?

1 John 1:7 _____

Isaiah 53:5 _____

(In my own pregnancies, my first response to any medical concerns was to receive communion.)

Personal Application

Modern psychology extols the benefits of self-analysis. Why is God's gift of discernment (insight) more beneficial? (See Hebrews 4:12-13.)

_____

Do you have a problem or question you have been unable to get to the root of? Write it down and then ask God for the insight to look past the surface issue and understand the real need or the real fear.

_____

_____

_____

$\mathscr{F}$URTHER $\mathscr{D}$EVOTIONAL $\mathscr{R}$EADING

I Can Fill My Life with Praise

> Therefore by Him let us continually offer the sacrifice of praise to God, that is, the fruit of our lips, giving thanks to His name (Hebrews 13:15).

Also see Deuteronomy 8:10; 1 Chronicles 16:25; Psalm 9:11; 33:2; 35:28; 67:3; 113:3; Acts 2:46-47; Colossians 3:15-17; 1 Thessalonians 5:18; Hebrews 13:15; 1 Peter 2:9

I Can Speak by Faith

> Whoever says to this mountain, "Be removed and be cast into the sea," and does not doubt in his heart, but believes that those things he says will be done, he will have whatever he says (Mark 11:23).

Also see Mark 11:23-24; John 16:23-24; 1 John 3:21-22; 5:14-15

God Will Give Me Insight and Discernment

> If any of you lacks wisdom, let him ask of God, who gives to all generously and without reproach, and it will be given to him (James 1:5).

Also see Ecclesiastes 2:26; 7:19; Psalm 25:14; Isaiah 11:2; Daniel 2:20-21; Luke 21:15; 2 Timothy 3:14-15

Summary

For the first time in your pregnancy, your baby is making you continually aware of his or her presence. The fetus has gained weight and increased in size so that you now have the pleasure of feeling the stir of life within.

At the same time, are you allowing God to add weight to your spiritual life? Are you understanding the power in scriptural practices such as positive confession, praise, and communion?

Every woman is concerned about looking attractive during her pregnancy, and today you can enjoy the blessing of flattering maternity outfits. But in this chapter, we have not been considering outward appearance but spiritual sight—God's "ultrasound." Don't forget about the lovely clothing that is available for your spirit! God will give us...

Beauty for ashes; joy instead of mourning;
praise instead of heaviness.

ISAIAH 61:3

Things
My Doctor
Told Me This Month...

_____

_____

_____

_____

_____

_____

My Physical Changes...

_____

_____

_____

Things
I've Thought
About This Month...

_____

_____

_____

_____

_____

_____

My Special Verse...

_____

_____

_____

The Seventh Month

Your baby's weight has almost doubled since last month. The fetus is now longer than your uterus, so he or she has to assume the fetal position of head to chest. Your baby's skin is wrinkled and red, but fatty tissue begins to form beneath it. During this last trimester, the fetus receives immunity to many germs newborns encounter. Taste buds are well developed. Inside the scull, the brain is growing rapidly, and its sections begin to take on lifelong roles.

But now, O Lord, You

are our Father;

We are the clay, and

You are our potter;

And all we are the work

of Your hand.

ISAIAH 64:8

PREPARING A HOME

We should make our plans—
counting on God to direct us.
Commit your work to the Lord,
then it will succeed.
PROVERBS 16:9,3 TLB

When God created man in His image, He gave us the gifts of a free will and tremendous creative potential. At no time in life are creative decisions more fun than when you are preparing your home for a new baby! Though you may not fit into the category of a traditional "bootie knitter," in as many ways as possible you are busily building a nest for your soon-to-appear child.

God wants to be your Partner in the preparation! His Holy Spirit can work alongside you, assisting you with wise advice. While you are working through the following list of things to do and decisions to make, get to know the Lord as your Counselor! "His name will be called Wonderful, Counselor, Mighty God, Everlasting Father, Prince of Peace" (Isaiah 9:6).

Prepared Childbirth Training

Both you and your husband will profit from attending some type of childbirth training course, which usually begins in this seventh month. Whether your delivery is completely natural or aided by anesthesia, fear will dissolve as you understand the entire birth process. Labor will be much easier with the help of relaxing exercises and breathing techniques. The wise woman is the one who is well prepared for what lies ahead (see Proverbs 27:12).

The classes will also empower your husband to strengthen you through labor and delivery and share the indescribably poignant moment of the birth of your child. "Two are better than one...and a threefold cord is not quickly broken" (Ecclesiastes 4:9,12). This verse is often used to explain the strength of a man, his wife, and the presence of the Lord. Your husband and your Lord will be the constant companions who unite with you to bring your child into the world.

Now is also the time to understand the medical options and to talk with your doctor so that you understand terms such as *episiotomy* and *epidural.*

Child-Care Preparation

If your experience with infants is lacking, you may not be as concerned about delivery as you are about caring for the baby when you bring him or her home. Don't panic! Use the next few weeks to give yourself a crash course on the care of infants. Many community groups, such as the Red Cross, offer brief yet excellent classes. Now is also the time to purchase a reliable child-care book.

(Be sneaky: look up steps A, B, and C for those questions you feel too embarrassed to ask anyone, such as "What really is the best way to bathe an infant?")

Best of all, expose yourself to the real thing! Visit friends with babies or volunteer for a few turns in the church nursery or day-care center. "Get all the [godly] advice you can and be wise the rest of your life" (Proverbs 19:20 TLB). "In a multitude of counselors, there is safety" (Proverbs 24:6).

The Nursery and Layette

Your head will swim as you look over the list of suggested baby furniture and clothing. Where do you begin? What guidelines does the Word of God offer for this part of your preparation?

You'll love assembling a soft, tiny wardrobe, choosing baby furniture, and working with your husband to repaint that fantastic "find" you made at a garage sale (with lead-free paint, of course!). Enjoy every moment!

But don't go overboard—baby will quickly outgrow the wee shirts and gowns; and *convenient and durable,* instead of super-deluxe, should be the standard for nursery equipment.

Because of my own Native American heritage, I have always loved the tradition of the beaded and decorated cradle boards that the mother, grandmother, and aunties made for each papoose. I once visited my friend Molly of the Paiute nation as she struggled to finish the beadwork on a cradle board (in spite of her full-term figure). I came home more thankful for modern simplicity—and glad that I had only chosen to prepare tiny mocassins!

Your devotional reading for this month includes Proverbs' description of the model wife and mother. A major trait of her character is practical wisdom:

> She goes out to inspect [each purchase before she] buys it...She is energetic, a hard worker, and watches for bargains...She watches carefully all that goes on throughout her household and is never lazy (Proverbs 31:16-18,27).

Practical wisdom is the natural outworking of true spiritual wisdom! The Lord literally wants to teach you to profit (see Isaiah 48:17).

"Remember, your Father knows exactly what you [and your unborn child] need even before you ask him" (Matthew 6:8 TLB). Luke adds this promise:

> [Don't] be of anxious (troubled) mind [unsettled, excited, worried, and in suspense]...your Father knows [what] you need...Only aim at...and seek after His kingdom, and all these things shall be supplied to you also (Luke 12:29-31 AMP).

In a modern world that is flooded with advertisements, we can easily become unrealistic and materialistic. We can develop an inflated idea of what possessions we need for ourselves or for our children. First Timothy 6:6 uses a word that we seldom hear anymore and even more seldom see personified. It is the word *contentment.* "Godliness with contentment is great gain." If you want to give true wealth to your baby's home, pray about the rare personality traits of contentment and peace.

Acquaint Yourself with Hospital Procedures

Now is the time to find answers to any questions you have about what to do when the big moment arrives. The hospital where you plan to deliver will gladly welcome you and your husband on a tour of the maternity ward. Usually, you can fill out admittance forms ahead of time just in case your infant comes quickly. Find out about billing procedures so that financial red tape will not distract you from enjoying your newborn. Claim the promise that "God shall supply all your need according to His riches in glory" (Philippians 4:19).

If you wish to have "rooming in" privileges, make arrangements in advance. Find out when and how your physician wishes to be notified when labor begins. Have the phone numbers of your doctor and close relatives handy, and be ready to call the special Christian friends who have agreed to support you in prayer throughout the birth.

If you are planning to deliver in your own home, having everything ready with ample time to spare is especially important. The majority of babies are born within three days of the estimated due date, but your child could always come early.

Have you arranged to have help during the first days with your tiny infant? Whether you choose a relative or a neighbor, this blessed person may not do everything the way you would, but receive her help gladly. Scripture teaches older women to teach the younger women.

Nursing or Formula

Today most physicians recommend breast feeding—it's the healthiest, most economical, and easiest way to feed your infant. The Lord has marvelously equipped you to provide your baby with a diet that is precisely balanced nutritionally, is easily digestible, and provides a definite immunity to childhood diseases. In Bible times, children were often nursed for several years. Isaiah 66:11 compares a time of peace in Israel with the tremendous comfort a baby receives from nursing at his mother's breast.

You may run into a few complications, the most common being a slowing of your milk supply or the letdown reflex due to emotional or physical stress. In previous chapters you have already encountered the remedy for an emotional crisis: Take it straight to prayer!

Purchase a guide to breast feeding (Karen Pryor's *Nursing Your Baby* is excellent, and your medical professional may offer a free handbook). Be sure to be well-read *before* you hold that hungry little person in your arms! If you begin now, you'll be ready to nurse your child.

Unfortunately, breast feeding is not only common, some women advocate it with religious fervor, preaching that it is the answer for everyone. If for some reason, such as a return to work, you decide to use formula, *do not feel condemned*. Remember, the love and cherishing you give your baby is far more important than the source of his or her milk!

An Atmosphere of Love

More crucial than the physical environment that surrounds your children is the emotional environment of your home. A stable, secure home life flows from a stable, secure marriage. The best way to prepare your nest, far more important than preparing a room, is to strengthen that love relationship.

Don't try to place on a child the heavy responsibility of "bringing you closer." If you have had problems communicating, if you have hurts or misunderstandings to deal with, work through them *before* your baby arrives. Pray for strength because children will place greater demands on your union. Perhaps you need to consider seeking help from your pastor or other experienced counselors. If you seek counsel, remember to seek the advice of *godly* advisers.

Even the best of marriages will profit from some of the excellent and readily available books on the Christ-centered marriage. Determine to grow in your relationship with the partner God has given you, even as you have determined to grow in your relationship with

Him! Love in marriage can be continually refreshed, for love springs from God. Ecclesiastes 9:9 tells us that we can learn to live joyfully all the days of our life with the partner we chose in our youth.

With zest and enthusiasm, you can face the creative challenge of preparing the nest. God is our Creator, the true source of all creativity, and He has made us in His image. We can ask Him to help us be creative.

Commit your work to the Lord, then it will succeed.

PROVERBS 16:3 TLB

$\mathcal{F}$AITH $\mathcal{B}$UILDERS

The Scriptural Principles

What will ensure the stability of the home you are preparing for your baby? (See Matthew 7:25; 1 Corinthians 3:11.)

_____

_____

Your marriage relationship will be strengthened as you follow God's scriptural instructions. What challenge does Paul give to wives in Ephesians 5:22-24 and Titus 2:4-5?

_____

_____

We are to honor our husbands for the protection of our marriages, not because we are inferior. What is the even more sobering challenge given to husbands? (See Ephesians 5:25,28; 1 Peter 3:7.)

_____

Personal Application

Proverbs 31 describes a woman whose children and husband praise her (see verse 28). Translate into modern terms the practical ways she cares for her family.

_____

_____

_____

_____

_____

According to Proverbs 21:9 and 25:24, what is the most destructive trait a wife can have?

_____

According to 1 Samuel 3:13, why did God judge Eli's house?

_____

What effect can your life have on your family's faith? (See 1 Peter 3:1-2.)

_____

List some ways you can strengthen your marriage.

_____

_____

_____

Make this a matter of continuing prayer throughout the month.

Practical Preparation

What two extremes should you avoid as you prepare your nest?

Proverbs 6:6-8; 18:9 _____

Matthew 6:19; 1 Timothy 6:10 _____

Extravagance and overspending may point to insecurity—see Hebrews 13:5. Now is the perfect time to memorize 1 Timothy 6:6: "Godliness with contentment is great gain."

Do you feel lacking in creative ability? Are you concerned that you don't know how to do many things, such as sewing and decorating? Study Exodus 31:3-5. Where did these artisans get their ability?

_____

What is one way the Lord will provide your baby with material blessings? (See Isaiah 48:17.)

_____

$\mathcal{F}$URTHER $\mathcal{D}$EVOTIONAL $\mathcal{R}$EADING

God Will Provide for My Needs

> And my God shall supply all your need according to
> His riches in glory by Christ Jesus (Philippians 4:19).

Also see Job 38:41; Psalm 23:5; 31:19; 78:20; 145:15-16; Isaiah 30:23; Malachi 3:10; Ephesians 3:20-21

We Can Build a Solid Home

> Two are better than one, Because they have a good
> reward for their labor. For if they fall, one will lift up
> his companion…Again, if two lie down together, they
> will keep warm…Though one may be overpowered by
> another, two can withstand him. And a threefold cord is
> not quickly broken (Ecclesiastes 4:9-12).

Also see Genesis 2:24; Deuteronomy 4:9; Proverbs 18:22; Song of Solomon 8:7; Colossians 3:19; 1 Timothy 3:4; 5:4; Titus 2:4-5; Hebrews 13:4

Summary

God is your Partner as you prepare your home for the new baby. One of the Old Testament names of God is Jehovah Jireh, which means "the Lord will provide." "Your Father knows the things you have need of before you ask Him" (Matthew 6:8). And He knows what things your newborn child will need as well!

The wise woman builds her house...
Through wisdom a house is built,
and by understanding it is established;
By knowledge the rooms are filled
With all precious and pleasant riches.

PROVERBS 14:1; 24:3-4

Things
My Doctor
Told Me This Month...

_____

_____

_____

_____

_____

_____

_____

My Physical Changes...

_____

_____

_____

Things
I've Thought
About This Month...

_____

_____

_____

_____

_____

_____

My Special Verse...

_____

_____

_____

The Eighth Month

Your baby can weigh as much as five pounds, measuring 16 to 18 inches. Everything in your baby's body is preparing for his or her entry into the world. Lungs develop strength, skin is not so wrinkled but still red, and limbs grow plump. Protective covering *(vernix caseosa)* waterproofs the infant's skin. Fingernails may have grown past the tiny fingertips. If your baby is a boy, his testicles have nearly completed their descent. And although the child within doesn't actually breathe, he or she does make breathing movements to practice for the real thing and occasionally even gets the hiccups!

You gave me skin

and flesh and knit together

bones and sinews.

You gave me life

and were so kind and loving to me,

and I was preserved by your care.

JOB 10:11-12 TLB

REFINING AND REFLECTION

Cast your burden upon the LORD,
And He shall sustain you.

PSALM 55:22

*Let patience have its perfect work, that you
may be perfect and complete, lacking nothing.*

JAMES 1:4

𝒪n these final weeks, your body is growing weary of the physical pressure of the child inside you.

You are exhausted from the effort of getting your cumbersome form out of bed, off of the sofa, or (cringe!) behind the wheel of your compact car. You're tired of not being able to sit close to the table, and you're sick of washing countless food stains off your protruding maternity tops.

You're tired of waddling instead of walking. Of getting up a dozen times each night to go to the bathroom. Of not being able to breathe deeply. Of skin stretched so tight it's painful. Of not being able to bend over and buckle your shoes. In fact, you'd be happy if you could even look down and see your shoes!

You've actually begun to wonder if the baby inside will ever come out!

Those who have never experienced the final months of a pregnancy laughingly misunderstand your fear that labor will *never* begin. You may think no one understands how you are feeling. Remember that you have an understanding heavenly Father. In Isaiah 66:9 (TLB), He reassures you, " 'Shall I bring to the point of birth and then not deliver?' asks the Lord your God. 'No! Never!' "

In these "pressing" days before delivery, as you faithfully go through your breathing exercises and relaxing drills, be faithful in exercising the spiritual quality of *patience*. "When the way is rough, your patience has a chance to grow. So let it grow... For when your patience is finally in full bloom, then you will be ready for anything, strong in character, full and complete" (James 1:3-4 TLB).

Complete. You're anxious for the arrival of your infant, but the work of the Holy Spirit is not yet completed!

You will never again have the joy of carrying *this* child inside you. Each succeeding pregnancy will be different. In the way your baby moves, kicks, and lays within you, he or she is already a unique individual. Each day is an opportunity for the Holy Spirit to whisper something new to your heart about this special little person.

For years, scientists have tried to discover the answer to the question, what causes labor to begin? The theories are varied. Is it a hormone produced by the mother? A hormone from the glands of the baby? Or could it be the involuntary reaction of the abdominal muscles that have held the baby for as long as possible? Doctors are still unable to pinpoint or even guess when your labor will begin.

God alone knows your true due date. In His omniscience, he has specifically ordained "a time to be born" (Ecclesiastes 3:2). In these last few days, He's adding a few finishing touches to the masterpiece you will soon hold in your arms. Don't be discouraged if baby overshoots his estimated time of arrival. Your child may need a little more nutrition, a little more stamina. Like your spiritual growth, the physical growth of the child inside you must be "complete, lacking nothing."

The last weeks of pregnancy are full of contradictions. You may want to hold your baby now and not a minute later, and yet you may be growing more fearful of labor. Some women report that they have more dreams than ever before during the last weeks of pregnancy (perhaps because sleep is so often interrupted). And it seems that people giving advice come out of the woodwork at this time, even with old wives' tales and myths about how to get your labor started! (In this time of New Age thinking, some of your neighbors may prove to be what was known in our grannies' day as *superstitious!*) If ever you needed a healthy sense of humor, it's now!

Since your baby has well-developed hearing at this time, let him or her hear the wonderful sound of your laughter! Proverbs 17:22 tells us that "a merry heart does good, like medicine." Take a moment to laugh about the funny moments of pregnancy.

One day in the eighth month of my third pregnancy, I stood in my living room, telling my mother how I could "hardly move at all." We were watching my four-year-old daughter outside the front window, when somehow my two-year-old son climbed into our car in the driveway, pulled off the emergency brake, and shifted into neutral, "driving" the car as it rolled backward into the street. I am still teased about how the woman who "couldn't move" suddenly ran out of the house, crossed the lawn, and *hurdled* both a short fence and a large bush to get to the toddler in the car! I had never hurdled anything in my life! My neighbor made me an award that read…"Gold Medal—Pregnant Olympics."

No time in life need be wasted—not even your final weeks as a woman in waiting. How can this time be fulfilling? As the Lord

Psalm 37

Verse 1—*"Do not fret."*
Review the Scriptures that calm your fear and anxiety (see "The Fourth Month").

Verse 3—*"Trust in the LORD, and do good."*
Your "good work" is to complete the preparation of your home and marriage for the birth of your infant (see "The Seventh Month").

Verse 4—*"Delight yourself also in the LORD."*
"Seek first the kingdom of God" (Matthew 6:33) by feeding your spirit through prayer and the Word (see "The Second Month").

Verse 5—*"Commit your way to the LORD."*
Experience the sweetness of welcoming His will, knowing that His will flows out of His love (see "The First Month").

Verse 7—*"Rest in the LORD, and wait patiently for Him."*
Carry through on your self-discipline; stay physically rested. You will need a storehouse of strength for your labor, which may begin at any time (see "The Fifth Month").

Verse 8—*"Cease from anger."*
Instead of accepting emotional turmoil, claim emotional stability…even when someone offers strange advice! Reign as a queen! (See "The Third Month".)

Verse 34—*"Keep his way."*
The Living Bible says, "Keep traveling steadily along his pathway." Allow the Lord to continually increase your spiritual insight and wisdom (see "The Sixth Month").

brings to completion your baby's physical preparation for birth and your spiritual preparation for motherhood, you can look to Psalm 37 for your assignment. Read this Psalm each morning (and perhaps memorize a portion of this passage); it is an excellent summary of all we have covered in this study guide.

Yes, dear sister, pregnancy at full term is a time of pressure. (Literally!) But times of pressure can be our times of greatest inner growth. They are times of refining, and…

There is wonderful joy ahead, even though the going is rough for a while… Trials are only to test your faith, to see whether or not it is strong and pure. It is being tested as fire tests gold and purifies it—and your faith is far more precious to God than mere gold.

1 PETER 1:6-7 TLB

He knows the way that I take;
when He has tested me,
I shall come forth as gold.

JOB 23:10

Faith Builders

The Gift of Patience
How does the first phrase of Psalm 37:7 define patience?

_____

_____

When we are involved in pressure situations, we always long for a way out! Why does the Lord allow times of pressure? (See Hebrews 12:1-2.)

_____

What will be the result of the trials or tests that come our way? There are several!

2 Corinthians 1:3-4 _____

Isaiah 48:10 _____

Hebrews 12:11 _____

The Amazing Truth
Besides the final weeks of pregnancy, are there any other pressing situations in your life you need to deal with at this time?

_____

_____

At times you may say, "I don't feel like I'm able to cope with this situation." Gain confidence as you study 1 Corinthians 10:13. (Paraphrase it here.)

_____

_____

The amazing truth is that times of pressure can bring our greatest spiritual growth. Trace the four steps of growth listed in Romans 5:3-5.

_____

_____

In These Last Days of Pregnancy

Which of the instructions of Psalm 37 is your greatest challenge?

_____

Read the promises of 1 John 5:14 and Matthew 21:22, and write a prayer about your challenge.

_____

_____

_____

_____

$\mathscr{F}$URTHER $\mathscr{D}$EVOTIONAL $\mathscr{R}$EADING

God Knows My Due Date

> You are He who took me out of the womb (Psalm 22:9).

Also see Psalm 22:10; 71:6; Galatians 1:15

I Can Be Content

> O LORD, You are the portion of my inheritance and
> my cup;
> You maintain my lot.
> The lines have fallen to me in pleasant places;
> Yes, I have a good inheritance (Psalm 16:5-6).

Also see Psalm 116:7; Isaiah 28:12; Jeremiah 6:16; Matthew 11:28-30;
Luke 3:14; 1 Timothy 6:6-8

I Can Be Patient

> The fruit of the Spirit is…patience (Galatians 5:22 NIV).

Also see Ecclesiastes 7:8; Luke 21:19; Colossians 1:11; 1 Thessalonians
5:14; Hebrews 6:15; James 1:3-4

Summary

Though you are still in a *waiting time,* no season of your life need be a *wasted time.*

The final days of your pregnancy can be a time of special instruction from the Lord. You will love the story of an expecting couple told in Judges 13:8-9:

> Then Manoah prayed to the LORD, and said, O my Lord…teach us what we shall do for the child who will be born. And God listened to the voice of Manoah.

Through his Holy Spirit, the Lord does speak to Christian mothers who seek Him. Allow your response to parallel Mary's:

> But Mary kept all these things and pondered them in her heart (Luke 2:19).

Things
My Doctor
Told Me This Month...

_____

_____

_____

_____

_____

_____

My Physical Changes...

_____

_____

_____

Things
I've Thought
About This Month...

_____

_____

_____

_____

_____

_____

My Special Verse...

_____

_____

_____

Delivery

At term, the infant averages four to eight and a half pounds. The bones of the head remain soft and flexible to enable the baby to pass through the birth canal. The child "drops," head in place, and is ready for birth. Labor may begin with contractions, mucus show, or rupture of the "bag of waters."

When you pass through the waters,

I will be with you.

ISAIAH 43:2

MY GREAT PHYSICIAN

You both precede and follow me
and place your hand of blessing on my head.

PSALM 139:5 TLB

I am holding you by your right hand—
I, the Lord your God—
and I say to you, Don't be afraid;
I am here to help you.

ISAIAH 41:13 TLB

*T*wo doctors will assist in the delivery of your new baby. One is your medical professional. The other is the One whom we know as the Great Physician.

What a comfort to understand that in addition to the hands of your doctor, God's gentle, loving spiritual hands will guide your baby down the birth canal and into your world! Two verses from the Psalms beautifully portray the role of the Lord in childbirth, especially if we look at these verses in the original language.

In Psalm 22:9-10, David said, "You are He who took me out of the womb... I was cast upon You from birth. From my mother's womb You have been my God." The word *took* in the New King James is translated from the Hebrew word *gazah,* meaning "to pull, or separate from; to cut." This verse pictures God as a skilled obstetrician, assisting in the birth, gently separating the baby from the mother and even cutting the umbilical cord.

In Psalm 71:6 we read, "By You I have been upheld from birth; You are He who took me out of my mother's womb." The verb *took* in this instance is the Hebrew word *qoach,* which means "working in a process to bring forth." God will work with you throughout your labor and delivery. The beginning of the verse shows an especially touching scene as the Great Physician holds up the newborn for the proud parents to see!

God is not only present when His daughters are in labor—He *understands* their labor and travail. Isaiah 42:14 tells us that *He has experienced birth pangs* as He endeavored to bring spiritual children into being. And for many of His children, the labor and delivery process is lengthy!

As a child of God, you are not living under a curse. During the Dark Ages, women were taught that God placed on Eve, and on all women, the curse of painful childbirth. This is not scriptural. In Genesis 3:16 we read this:

> To the woman He said: "I will greatly multiply your
> sorrow and your conception;
> In pain you shall bring forth children."

Once again, let's look to the original language for a clearer understanding of this verse. The word translated as *sorrow* in the New King James is the Hebrew word *esteb.* A much better translation of *esteb* would be "toil, labor, or very hard work." The same word is used in

Genesis 3:17, where God said to Adam, "In toil *[esteb]* you shall eat of it [the ground] all the days of your life." *Esteb* is translated as *toil* in other New King James verses, such as Genesis 5:29: "This one will comfort us concerning our work and the toil *[esteb]* of our hands."

God told Eve, "In labor, with toil and work, you will bring forth children."

Instead of fearing this new experience, realize that the Word says what lies ahead of you is just plain work! That's what the word *labor* means, isn't it? You will need strength to carry out your breathing techniques, strength to refrain from bearing down too soon, and strength to push when the right time arrives! The pains of labor are not the pains of an illness but rather the muscle pain of a great athletic undertaking, with the greatest of all rewards.

Below is a general guide for the progression of labor, but the wise woman is mentally prepared for the *variations* labor can bring. Your labor may be relatively short or considerably long. The pangs may center in your abdomen or in your lower back. You may feel an almost uncontrollable urge to push, or you may not feel the urge at all. You may deliver naturally, as planned, or decide to use mild anesthesia. The doctor may even decide to do a C-section. Though you have much in common with other women in waiting, your labor and delivery will be as unique as is the baby within you!

The First Stage of Labor

Effacement and dilation—*cervix is thinning and opening.*

Physical signs and changes

- ∾ pink or red vaginal mucous "show"
- ∾ possible back ache
- ∾ possible rupture of membranes

- ∾ regular uterine contractions increasing in strength, frequency, and duration.

Emotions

- ∾ excitement
- ∾ anticipation
- ∾ joy
- ∾ an energetic attitude

Your role

- ∾ Begin to breathe with contractions.
- ∾ Remain calm as you are admitted and prepped.
- ∾ Use relaxation drills (entire body).
- ∾ Change position every half hour.
- ∾ Empty bladder every half hour.
- ∾ Rest as much as possible between contractions.
- ∾ Rejoice! You're finally going to receive the gift of your baby!

Husband or coach's role

- ∾ Notify the doctor.
- ∾ At his instructions, take your wife to the hospital.
- ∾ Notify prayer partners and nearby relatives (if you have time!).
- ∾ Make sure your wife is comfortable.
- ∾ Reassure her and give encouragement.
- ∾ Remind her to change positions and empty bladder.
- ∾ Place a cool cloth on her forehead and touch ice to her lips (most hospitals won't allow her to drink water).
- ∾ Rub her back and give sacral pressure if that is helpful.
- ∾ Check with nurses on the progression of labor after each exam.

- Pray for her in a quiet voice.
- Read verses that have become special to her during the pregnancy.

Promises to claim:

- The LORD will give strength to His people; The LORD will bless His people with peace (Psalm 29:11).
- I will go in the strength of the Lord GOD (Psalm 71:16).

Transition

Cervix is dilating from seven to ten centimeters.

Physical signs and changes

- increasingly strong contractions
- possible backache and soreness of abdomen
- nausea
- weariness
- urge to push
- cheeks flushed (malar flush)
- chills

Emotions

- At three to four centimeters you become more serious and may no longer wish to talk.
- At eight to ten centimeters it is harder to concentrate.
- You may feel apprehension or fatigue.
- You may become irritable.

Your role

- Use transitional breathing drills.

- Practice relaxation drills (of abdominal wall); rely on your coach for help.
- Rest whenever possible (the nurse may offer a small dose of pain medication to help relaxation).
- Continue to change positions and empty bladder frequently.
- Claim God's peace and remember God's presence!

Husband or coach's role

- Time the contractions and deal with each one as it begins.
- Direct breathing and relaxation drills (breathe with her) and remind her to breathe deeply between contractions.
- Try backrub or sacral pressure. Encourage her and assure her she's doing well.
- Act as a go-between for the woman in labor and the staff; protect her from confusion. Get socks and blankets if she is chilly.
- Be willing to back off if she no longer wants to be touched.
- Tell nurses when she feels the urge to push; encourage her if she must wait.
- Continue to intercede for her and the baby.

A promise to claim

- I am holding you by your right hand—
  I, the Lord your God—
  and I say to you, Don't be afraid;
  I am here to help you (Isaiah 41:13 TLB).

Pushing

At the beginning of the second stage of labor, the mother cooperates with uterine muscles to push the baby down the birth canal.

Physical signs and changes

- ◌ tremendous urge to push
- ◌ pressure of baby's head in vagina
- ◌ feeling of warmth
- ◌ possible body trembling

Emotions

- ◌ relief that now you can push
- ◌ drowsy between contractions
- ◌ excitement again builds

Your role

- ◌ Assume the pushing position, take two deep breaths, take one more, hold and bear down.
- ◌ Cooperate with your doctor. If you need to temporarily refrain from pushing, use a panting drill.
- ◌ Rest between contractions.
- ◌ Rely on the Lord for His strength.

Husband or coach's role

- ◌ Hold up your wife's shoulders if supports aren't available.
- ◌ Remind her to relax between pushes. Breathe with her and comfort her.
- ◌ Tell her how well she's doing—cheer her on!

A promise to claim

- ∞ I can do all things through Christ who strengthens me (Philippians 4:13).

Delivery of the Child!

Physical signs and changes

- ∞ "pins and needles" sensation as vulva stretches
- ∞ birth outlet becomes numbed (doctor may give a local anesthetic)
- ∞ discomfort becomes less than it was during transition and pushing

Emotions

- ∞ excitement, yet peace
- ∞ laughing or crying with joy, awe, and reverence

Your role and your husband's role

- ∞ Watch for the baby's birth and enjoy it! Your difficult work is over!
- ∞ Encourage one another.
- ∞ Listen for the first cry!

Delivery of Placenta

At this third stage of labor, the placenta separates from the uterine wall and moves down the birth canal.

Physical signs and changes

- ∞ one or more final contractions
- ∞ stitches are taken to close episiotomy
- ∞ you may feel hunger or thirst as soon as task is completed

Emotions

- ‿ tremendous joy
- ‿ excited talking
- ‿ wide-awake feeling with renewed energy

Your role

- ‿ Cuddle and enjoy your newborn (many hospitals suggest nursing immediately).
- ‿ Thank your husband or coach for all the help.
- ‿ Thank the doctors and nurses.
- ‿ Praise and thank the Lord!
- ‿ Settle down for peaceful sleep.

Husband or coach's role

- ‿ Congratulate the new mom for a job well done.
- ‿ Hold and enjoy the new baby.
- ‿ Praise and thank the Lord.
- ‿ See Mom to the recovery room.
- ‿ Make important announcement phone calls.
- ‿ Get some well-earned rest.

Your weeping shall suddenly be turned to wonderful joy [when you see me again]. It will be the same joy as that of a woman in labor when her child is born—her anguish gives place to rapturous joy and the pain is forgotten.

JOHN 16:20-21 TLB

ℱᴀɪᴛʜ ℬᴜɪʟᴅᴇʀs

(This month, be sure to do the Bible study early!)

ℳy help comes from the LORD.

PSALM 121:2

What does God's Word promise regarding…

His presence in time of need? (See Psalm 41:2; 145:18.)

_____

The amount of strength available to us? (See Deuteronomy 33:25.)

_____

Prepared Childbirth classes encourage women to imagine a peaceful scene to facilitate relaxation in labor. Describe a scene Isaiah 40:31 brings to your mind.

_____

What help do these verses suggest God will give you in labor? Study the divine help available in labor with regard to:

2 Timothy 1:7 _____

Isaiah 28:12 _____

Jeremiah 30:17 _____

I am the LORD *who heals you.*

EXODUS 15:26

As a daughter of the Lord you are promised protection and safety. What do each of the following verses tell you about God's will for your physical well-being?

Psalm 103:3-4 _____

Isaiah 58:8 _____

Does the health promised to you apply to your baby as well?

Deuteronomy 28:1-11 (especially verse 4) _____

Psalm 107:15 _____

How does your Father respond to your prayers for your child? (See Isaiah 45:11.)

_____

In your own words, describe the picture given in Deuteronomy 33:12 of the way God will care for your infant.

_____

By a new and living way...

HEBREWS 10:20

As your contractions begin, remember that you are not bound to repeat the experiences of your mother, sister, or friends. What advice does Isaiah 43:18-19 give to the woman in labor?

_____

Earlier in this chapter you read that you are not under a curse in child-birth. What exciting truth do we find in 2 Corinthians 5:17-19?

_____

Further Devotional Reading

God Will Provide Me with Safety, Strength, and Protection

> As the mountains surround Jerusalem,
> So the LORD surrounds His people
> From this time forth and forever (Psalm 125:2).

Deuteronomy 33:12; Psalm 28:6-8; 33:17-22; 34:7-8; 91:1-16; Isaiah 30:15; 40:31; 41:10,13; John 10:10; 1 Timothy 2:15

God's Will Is for My Health

> Bless the LORD, O my soul,
> And forget not all His benefits:
> Who forgives all your iniquities,
> Who heals all your diseases,
> Who crowns you with lovingkindness (Psalm 103:2-4).

Psalm 107:20; Isaiah 53:5; Malachi 4:2; Matthew 10:8; Luke 9:2; 10:9; Acts 10:38; 1 Corinthians 12:9; James 5:14-16; 1 Peter 2:24

$\mathcal{S}$UMMARY

One of the titles the Word gives to the Lord Jesus parallels the experience that culminates your time as a woman in waiting—delivery. In Romans 11:26, as well as in many other beautiful portions of Scripture, we are told "The Deliverer will come."

Your Lord will be present as your Deliverer, your Great Physician. He is with you not only to help you but also to rejoice with you!

$\mathcal{T}$he Lord your God in your midst,
The Mighty One, will save,
He will rejoice over you with gladness
He will rejoice over you with singing.

ZEPHANIAH 3:17

Things
My Doctor
Told Me This Month...

_____

_____

_____

_____

_____

_____

My Physical Changes...

_____

_____

_____

Things
I've Thought
About This Month...

_____

_____

_____

_____

_____

_____

_____

My Special Verse...

_____

_____

_____

The Newborn

I have called you by your name;

You are mine.

ISAIAH 43:1

THE FEMININE SIDE OF GOD

Can a woman forget her nursing child,
And not have compassion on
the son of her womb?
Surely, they may forget,
Yet will I not forget you.

ISAIAH 49:15

The same God who created the surging tides and pounding surf of the ocean also designed the woodlands through which sparkling streams whisper His praise. The same God who raised the mighty redwood also stooped to fashion the pastel alpine edelweiss. The same God who shouted the rugged Rockies into existence also molded gently rolling moors. The same God who made man in His image also made woman.

The spectrum of creation points to two aspects of God's nature: that which is strongly masculine and that which is reminiscent of femininity.

Before delivery, you studied Scriptures that showed that the Lord identifies with a woman's labor and birth pains. Now that you have stepped into the challenge of motherhood, you'll find that the Word has much more to say about the "mothering" attributes of the Godhead.

- He knows how to comfort a crying infant (Isaiah 66:13).
- He understands about nursing and feeding a child (Hosea 11:4).
- He is sympathetic with a baby's needs (Psalm 103:13).
- He even knows the feeling of teaching a child to walk (Hosea 11:3).

In Luke 13:34, we catch a glimpse of the heart of God when Jesus cried, "O Jerusalem, Jerusalem!…How often I have wanted to gather your children together even as a hen protects her brood under her wings" (TLB).

By seeing the Scriptures' portrait of the tenderness of the Lord, you will grow to understand the special divine presence that is with a mother as she cares for her baby. The Bible has a beautifully descriptive word for God's tenderness. It is *loving-kindness.*

In loving-kindness, He is there to laugh with you as the nursing newborn tries to gobble you up! In loving-kindness, He is there to encourage you as you change diapers and wash clothes again and again.

Let us not lose heart and grow weary and faint in
acting nobly and doing right (Galatians 6:9 AMP).

In loving-kindness, He is there to stand guard with you as you
take the night watch over a sick or restless baby.

I meditate on You in the night watches (Psalm 63:6).

In loving-kindness, He is there to uphold you as you stumble to the
nursery in the dim light of dawn for that early-morning feeding.

I can't even count how many times a day your thoughts
turn toward me. And when I waken in the morning, you
are still thinking of me! (Psalm 139:17-18 TLB).

At times you may be troubled by ambivalence, a dividing of the
emotions, during this postpartum period. You love cuddling and
feeding your baby, but sometimes you feel overwhelmed by the
magnitude of your responsibility.

Sandy, one mother of a newborn, asked, "I'm adjusting well to the
responsibility, but I wonder if something is wrong with me. I don't
feel the surge of love that I expected to feel for my baby." If this has
troubled you, remember that love is not only emotion—it is action.
It includes a simple exercising of the will. Love is another step in
the walk of faith. By faith, care for your newborn lovingly, and the
surge of feeling will soon follow. After all, the newborn may look
like a little stranger in spite of the fact that he or she was inside you
for nine months! In a few short days, you will wholeheartedly say,
"This is bone of my bone and flesh of my flesh."

Both you and your husband will deal with some feelings of
selfishness. Even when you have carefully planned for and dearly
wanted your child, your style of living can't help but be interrupted.

Will we ever be able to do all those things we want to do? you wonder. *What about the sacrifices of time and money we will be making for our children?*

Don't feel condemned by these thoughts—they simply mean that you see parenthood as reality and not just a fantasy. When troubled, remind yourself of the kingdom principle of *great gain through giving.*

In Matthew 10:39, Jesus told His disciples, "If you cling to your life, you will lose it; but if you give it up for me, you will save it" (TLB). He meant that some of those listening would lose their lives because of their faith and discover the greater treasure of eternal salvation. This verse can also apply to the quality of life you will find as you give yourself in service, for in Luke 6:38 (TLB) He said this:

> For if you give, you will get! Your gift will return to you in full and overflowing measure, pressed down, shaken together to make room for more, and running over. Whatever measure you use to give—large or small—will be used to measure what is given back to you.

Mothering is the "givingest" task in the world, for the newborn baby cannot show a great deal of thanks. On the days when the job seems thankless, remember that as you give to your child, you are giving to the Lord. "If, as my representatives, you give even a cup of cold water to a little child, you will surely be rewarded" (Matthew 10:42 TLB). "When you did it [fed, helped, or clothed] to these my brothers you were doing it to me!" (Matthew 25:40 TLB).

God will add His blessing to the repetitive, routine tasks of motherhood. Jesus delighted in adding a miraculous touch to the everyday lives of everyday people...turning the commonplace into the extraordinary. He can turn water into wine! He can turn what would be daily drudgery into a school of joyful discipleship!

In addition to physical care, what spiritual care can you provide for your newborn child?

First of all, the name you chose for this baby was certainly meaningful to you and your husband. Our Jewish spiritual heritage assigns great significance to the names we choose for our children. Israeli boys' names often included *el,* which referred to the name of the Lord: Joel, Daniel, Michael. Girls' names were often taken from beautiful objects in nature. Rachel means "God's lamb."

Have you discovered verses from Scripture that add meaning to your child's name? Excellent reference books are available today, some even including a verse from the Bible that relates to each name. As you intercede for your infant, you can pray that the characteristics of your baby's name become reality. You can reasonably believe that your child's name is even God-given! We read of many instances in Scripture of God naming infants before they were born. To your special baby, the Lord can say what He said to Israel: "I have called you by your name; you are mine" (Isaiah 43:1).

Another important principle of spiritual care is your infant's dedication to the Lord. This can be done publicly (perhaps you have been present in church services when children were dedicated) or privately in your own home.

This is a time of verbally recognizing that this is God's child, a time of committing him to a loving heavenly Father, a time of asking for wisdom to raise him according to the plan of the Lord. In Israel, the first place parents took a newborn was to the house of the Lord for the ceremony of dedication. Like Hannah at the dedication of Samuel, we can say, *"For this child I prayed, and the Lord has granted me my petition which I asked of him. Therefore I also have lent him to the Lord; as long as he lives he shall be lent to the Lord"* (1 Samuel 1:27-28).

The promises of God's Word are yours for the asking.

This month's Bible study is one of the most exciting you will ever experience, for it deals with the blessings that are available to your children. The mother of faith can claim health, happiness, wisdom, and even prosperity for her little ones.

Most of all, you can claim for them the same abundant life you have discovered in the Lord Jesus.

I will pour My Spirit on your descendants,
And My blessing on your offspring;
They will spring up among the grass
Like willows by the watercourses.
One will say, "I am the Lord's";
Another will call himself by the name of Jacob;
Another will write with his hand,
"The LORD's."

ISAIAH 44:3-5

𝒯aith ℬuilders

God's Plan for My Baby

The Word is a treasure chest of knowledge, showing you how to raise the child God has given you. What do these verses teach you about God's plan for...

discipline (1 Samuel 3:13; Proverbs 19:18; 29:17)

_____

training by example (Proverbs 22:6; 2 Timothy 1:5)

_____

showing love and tenderness (Ephesians 6:4; Titus 2:4)

_____

spiritual teaching (Deuteronomy 6:7; Joshua 24:15)

_____

forgiveness (Luke 15:20-24)

_____

God's Hand on My Baby

You'll rejoice as you discover the heritage your child receives by being born in a godly home. What can you believe God for in each of the following areas?

material blessing (Psalm 37:25) _____

joy (Psalm 149:2) _____

truthfulness (Isaiah 63:8) _____

favor with people (Proverbs 20:7; 1 Samuel 2:26) _____

emotional strength (Isaiah 54:13) _____

salvation (Acts 2:39; 1 John 2:13) _____

"The Joy That a Human Being Has Been Born..." (John 16:21)

Your baby is a living illustration of God's blessing on your life. You have just studied the ways in which you are to give to your child. Now consider what the Word says your child will give to you!

Psalm 127:3 _____

Psalm 127:4_____

Psalm 127:5a_____

Psalm 127:5b_____

Proverbs 17:6_____

Proverbs 31:28 _____

A child can also have a spiritual impact on his parents! What did the children's actions teach in each of these instances?

2 Chronicles 24:1_____

1 Samuel 2:18_____

Matthew 21:15-16_____

In your journal, write a prayer request of how you desire this child to bring you joy in his lifetime. (For an example of prayer for a child's future, see 1 Chronicles 29:19.)

FURTHER DEVOTIONAL READING

I Can Dedicate My Children to the Lord

> O LORD of hosts, if You...will give Your maidservant
> a male child, then I will give him to the LORD all the days
> of his life (1 Samuel 1:11).

Also see Exodus 13:12; Numbers 3:13; Nehemiah 10:35-36; Luke 2:22

God Will Give Me Parental Love and Wisdom

> Do not provoke your children to wrath, but bring
> them up in the training and admonition of the Lord
> (Ephesians 6:4).

Also see Genesis 18:19; Psalm 78:3-8; 2 Timothy 1:5

The Birth of My
Child of Promise

Name: _____

Date and Time: _____

Place of Birth: _____

_____

_____

_____

_____

_____

Friends and Family Present: _____

_____

_____

_____

Special Memories of
My Baby's Birth and
First Few Days...

_____

_____

_____

_____

_____

_____

_____

_____

_____

_____

_____

_____

_____

Some days mothering is easy.
Some days it is not.
Always remember your Source.
As time goes by, recall these days
of spiritual preparation.
Reread your journal.
Review the Scriptures that became your own.
When you held your new baby,
you learned the reality of the phrase
"He will...gently lead those who are with young."
In the years to come
the promise will be completed:

He will gather the lambs with His arms.

ISAIAH 40:11

BIBLIOGRAPHY

American College of Obstetricians and Gynecologists. *Planning for Pregnancy, Birth and Beyond,* Second Edition. New York: Penguin Group USA Inc., 1997.

Ash, Jennifer and Armin Brott. *The Expectant Father.* New York: Abbeville Press, 200l.

Bradford, Nikki. *The World of Your Unborn Baby.* Chicago: McGraw Hill, 1998.

Brand, Paul and PhillipYancy. *Fearfully and Wonderfully Made.* Grand Rapids: Zondervan, 1980.

Bowker, John. *The Complete Bible Handbook.* London: Dorling Kindersley Limited, 1998.

Eisenber, Arlene and Heidi Murkoff. *What to Expect When You're Expecting.* New York: Workman Publishing, 1997.

Huggins, Kathleen. *The Nursing Mother's Companion.* Boston: Harvard Common Press, 2005.

Omartian, Stormie. *The Power of a Praying® Parent.* Eugene, OR: Harvest House, 1999.

Spangler, Ann and Jean Swerda. *The Mothers of the Bible.* Grand Rapids: Zondervan, 2001.

Vine, W.E. *An Expository Dictionary of Biblical Words.* Nashville: Thomas Nelson, 1985.

Zodhiates, Spiros. *The Complete WordStudy New Testament.* Chattanooga: AMG Publishers, 1991.

Other Great
Harvest House Books
for Moms

365 Things Every New Mom Should Know
Linda Danis

This daily guide to the first year of motherhood combines prayerful, playful, and practical information to energize new moms. It features weekly devotionals and daily activities that foster a baby's physical, emotional, social, and spiritual growth.

10-Minute Time Outs for Moms
Grace Fox

Insightful devotions from author and mother Grace Fox empower you to maintain a vital connection with God. Inspiring stories, Scripture-based prayers, and practical guidance offer you strength for your spiritual journey and daily life.

The Power of a Praying® Woman
Stormie Omartian

Stormie's deep knowledge of Scripture and candid examples from her own prayer life provide guidance as you trust God with your deepest longings and cover every area of your life with prayer.

A Baby Is a Gift from God

In this beautiful gift book, the cheery characters from the Land of Milk and Honey™ celebrate alongside joyous quotes to remind new parents, grandparents, and everyone else that a child is a gift straight from God's heart to their own.

A Baby to Love

An adorable lion, a fun goose, a delightful rabbit, and huggable bears make this baby memory book endearing. As a parent, you will find the engaging questions and insightful lead-in sentences fun to fill in. Includes cheery quotes on babyhood.